Breakfast may be the most important meal of the day, but it's also the most intimate and personal. It's when we're in our pyjamas and with our families, not quite ready to face the world. It's what we crave when we want comfort and it's the easiest way to turn us back into kids again.

Mark Pupo got into the habit of preparing big breakfasts every Sunday with his neurodivergent kindergartener, Sam. Everything else in life was tough and complicated, but making breakfast together was weirdly easy. (It turned out Sam loved to crack eggs, and he was really good at it.) In the kitchen, the pressure was off and they had all the time in the world to goof around. This book is a record of that first year of a father and son cooking together—of what became their weekend ritual.

Filled with playful illustrations and 52 recipes for a full year of weekend breakfasts, *Sundays* is a journey through Mark and Sam's morning adventures. Starting with simpler challenges, like Toast Soldiers and Almond Butter Overnight Oats, it builds to Mark's favourite inspired dishes, including Eggnog French Toast Bake, Pumpkin Spice Pancakes, Cheddar Polenta Cakes, and Saucy Poached Eggs with Feta. Mark also revisits his own childhood breakfast obsessions (Pop-Tarts, egg sandwiches, and the elusive perfect bagel, to name a few), and along the way explores the surprising origins of breakfast staples.

By turns witty, charming, frank, and filled with delicious breakfast ideas, this book is for anyone who wishes every morning began with a stack of pancakes. *Sundays* is an infectious celebration of the most important meal of the day and the most important people in our lives.

PRODUCT OF QU

REFRIGERATE AFTER OP

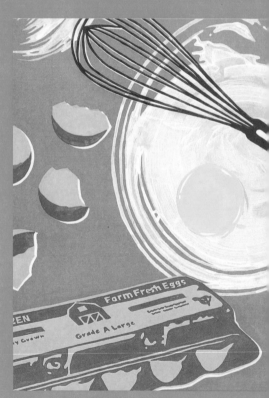

FarmFresh Eggs

Grade A Large

SUNDAYS

A Celebration of
Breakfast and Family in
52 Essential Recipes

MARK PUPO

appetite
by RANDOM HOUSE

Appetite by Random House® and colophon are registered trademarks of Penguin Random House LLC.

Library and Archives Canada Cataloguing in Publication is available upon request.
ISBN: 9780525611103
eBook ISBN: 9780525611110

Page vi: Permission granted to use excerpt from *Toast* by Nigel Slater
© Nigel Slater 2003
Page vi: Permission granted by the Literary Trust under the will of M.F.K. Fisher.

Interior design: Lisa Jager
Interior illustrations: Christopher Rouleau

Printed in China

Published in Canada by Appetite by Random House®, a division of Penguin Random House Canada Limited.

www.penguinrandomhouse.ca

10 9 8 7 6 5 4 3 2 1

For Sam and Stephen

"Probably one of the most private things
in the world is an egg until it is broken."

M.F.K. Fisher

"It's impossible not to love someone who makes toast for you."

Nigel Slater

CONTENTS

Good Morning!

The clerk at the salvage store said the table was originally a workbench. It was a foot and a half wide. The tabletop was a thick, two-inch oak board, cracked and dotted with drill holes from decades of carpentry projects. That's *character*, said the clerk. I tried to imagine myself sitting at this table, facing my husband, Stephen. We'd be the definition of face-to-face. Anyone not a fan of mealtime intimacy would be out of luck. But I noted how the table had curving iron legs and feet that splayed out like the paws of a plump Labrador. We lived downtown and our kitchen was narrow, so we needed an equally narrow table that could handle double duty as a prep surface. It was perfect.

Our new-but-old kitchen table is where we now unpack our groceries and chop vegetables. It's where we place boards of cheese, olives, and nuts when people come over and where, once a year, we end up organizing papers into piles when we do our taxes. It's our home base. If someone left their phone somewhere, or their keys, or their to-do list, that's where we look first. It's also, most importantly, our breakfast table.

Now that our son, Sam, is in elementary school and always interrupting us with new interests and quirks, every morning promises a new surprise too. The table's narrowness is a plus: we touch knees while we dig into our oatmeal or eggs. It's where we hash out the day's agenda. It's where we watch the sparrows and squirrels outside the kitchen window while they battle over seeds. It's where Sam hums along to the morning radio shows and I wait for the weather report. It's where everything starts.

A few years ago, around the time Sam graduated from mush to solids, I got into the habit of preparing big breakfasts every Sunday. We almost never had anything else scheduled on a Sunday. The pressure was off and we had all the time we wanted to goof around in the kitchen. Our ideal menu always included something savoury, something salty, something toasted, and something sweet. Some people like a simple breakfast—just toast or just porridge—but there's a lot to be said for what's called a well-rounded breakfast. Maybe porridge or cream of wheat to start, then eggs and bacon or sausage (or both), plus some fruit and toast. There should be good coffee and, in our household, a choice of fresh juice (since we each have our preferred kind, and Sam likes to mix them all together—what he calls his "rainbow juice"). For a finale, glazed danishes or maybe a croissant studded with toasted almonds. A still-warm, cakey doughnut won't last long.

My mom taught me how to cook when I was a teen, mostly by letting me figure it out for myself. Breakfast was my specialty. I worked my way through the *Joy of Cooking* (blintzes, Dutch babies, hushpuppies), then our collection of Silver Palate cookbooks (so many quiches!), then James Beard (puffed eggs, baked eggs with tomatoes, farmer's sausage), plus the buttermilk pancakes and cheddar biscuits in our free supermarket calendars. The hardest recipes to master were the most basic-seeming egg dishes—the perfect creamy omelette, the precisely timed poach, a custard-like scramble. Now that I'm a parent, I'm revisiting all those recipes for Sam, who has become an expert spotter of a pancake that's ready to be flipped—and delivered to his plate.

Breakfast is better together. Science says so. Researchers have proven that families who sit down for breakfast have better physical and mental health. Kids do better at school. And everyone lives longer. One Australian meta-analysis of health studies showed that people who skip breakfast experience an 87 percent increase in risk for death from cardiovascular disease—and a 19 percent increase in risk for all causes of death.

The sociologist Jean-Claude Kaufmann, trying to explain how and why we invest so much meaning in our cooking, noted how the family table was originally a sacrificial altar that evolved, as recently as the 17th century, into a place where we gather daily. Like all sociologists, he writes about his subjects like he's observing aliens, noting how "the data from [his] survey allowed [him] to confirm there is a very close relationship between families and meals." Who would dispute that?

Lunch is all about efficiency. Dinner is usually the most labour-intensive and expensive meal of the day. But it's breakfast that's the most intimate and personal. We eat breakfast in our pyjamas, sometimes still hazy with dreaming. You know someone loves you when they make you a big breakfast. It works the other way too: making a big breakfast for someone you love tastes just as good, if not best of all.

Family
and Sundays

My mornings were once so quick and simple, bordering on austere, you'd think I secretly wished I was a monk. A single slice of buttered toast. A shot of orange juice, maybe a few spoonfuls of yogurt if it was going to be a long day. Fill a mug with coffee, and on with it. Then, as can happen if you're not paying close attention, two people—my husband and my kid—took over my mornings. That was the end of that.

I met Stephen when we were in our early 30s. One of the first things I discovered is he's one of those people who lives—lives, lives, LIVES— for a long, leisurely breakfast. You can't rush him out a door. That was the first reason I had to recalibrate my morning pace. He's also a French toast-o-phile. If we're eating out for breakfast and there's French toast on the menu, he's set. At home on any given morning, he'll magically find a day-old baguette in the pantry, twist open a jar of vanilla paste, and start whipping eggs.

Stephen's not much of a talker, which must have something to do with growing up in a big Irish Catholic family in a Cape Breton coal mining town, always drowned out by his many louder siblings. Ten years into our relationship, he returned home from a trip to visit family out east and showed me photos of him posing with his nieces, who were at the time both under five. They were goofing around and he looked happy in a way I'd almost forgotten he could. So I asked, without any buildup or warning, if he wanted to have a kid. Okay, he said. He looked relieved. It was pretty clear he'd been waiting, with some impatience, for me to finally arrive at the idea.

A few years and many completed adoption-prep courses later, as I was sitting in a meeting at work, our Children's Aid caseworker sent an email: we'd been matched. I peeked up from my phone and tried to keep my face from showing too much of my excitement (the work meeting certainly didn't call for any). Our kid was still a baby—just six months old—and waiting at a foster home.

The night before we were to meet our matched baby for the first time, my brain swam with cribs, Jolly Jumpers, Diaper Genies, booster seats, Lego sets, parent-teacher meetings, lice checks, and crack-of-dawn hockey practices. We didn't even have a room prepared for a kid—did this mean I'd need to give up my home office? I'd somehow fooled myself into believing that adopting wouldn't change much in our lives. That it'd be a small tweak to our routines, like hosting a new if demanding houseguest. I'd also been avoiding thinking through all the real-world logistics of adopting a kid. Did we live in a good school district? Would we be able to choose a new name for him? What if, like some other kids adopted out of the public system, he came with needs, physical or mental, that were far beyond what we could handle?

The foster parents' home was in the suburbs, past the city zoo and at the end of a maze of curving crescents. We'd brought along a toy stuffed fox in a striped sweater. I froze at the door before ringing the bell and gave Stephen one last look. He tried for a brave grin. We were about to transform (would it be instant?) from duo to trio.

The foster couple had dressed the baby in a button-down shirt and a little wool vest. He was the definition of doll-like, with apple cheeks and big, curious eyes. This was only a short visit—we'd been warned it'd take a month of progressively longer sessions, including a sleepover at our house, before he'd come to live with us. We sat with the foster family in their living room, between pictures of all the kids they'd cared for over the last 20 years. Stephen and I took turns holding the baby, trying to figure out how to support his heavy head and chubby limbs. He squirmed a lot, seeming to want to get a better look at us.

I'm remembering this moment years later, trying to make sense of it. We took a few photos to capture our first meeting, and in every single one of them I look flushed, dizzy, and mildly panicked. It went by in a blur. But I know the exact instant we officially became parents was when our brand-new boy drifted asleep at 3:37 p.m. on March 29, 2017, in Stephen's arms. That's the timestamp of the photo I took with my phone. Stephen is smiling in the photo exactly like he did in those photos from years before, of him goofing around with his nieces.

Right then, at 3:37 p.m., it hit me: I was a dad. This kid was now my entire life. Everything else would have to wait.

We named him Sam.

Sam is the reason I'm writing this book. When I started working on it, he was four. And as anyone with a young child will explain between yawns, they're a lot of work. And a lot more each day. Sam especially. Because he's a lot of work, I've become very good at making breakfast. Fast breakfasts pulled in a few seconds from the fridge, slow breakfasts that require night-before mixing and planning, and every kind of breakfast in between. Most kids love breakfast, but Sam brings a special intensity to his love for breakfast. He'd eat breakfast all day long, if we let him. And now, come to think of it, so would I.

Every kid is special, but Sam goes the extra mile. He has never stopped being incredibly cute. Okay, okay, yes—I'd be a terrible parent if I didn't believe my kid was cute, but I swear to you that Sam can't take a bad photo, even mid-tantrum. When we started him in preschool, his classmates trailed after him like he was the lead singer in a boy band. When one of us took him out for a solo walk around our neighbourhood in his stroller, we'd always be stopped by strangers. People gush over babies all the time, but this was weird. I thought it was funny the first time an elderly gent said, unprompted, "Gee, his mom must be quite good looking." The second, third, and twentieth time that happened, I clocked the insult.

When Sam was nearing his second birthday, we worried that he was avoiding looking at us when we spoke. We'd say his name, then say it a bit louder, and then louder again, and he wouldn't react. His hearing was fine—our family doctor assured us he was physically perfect (see! I wasn't the only one who thought so!). But he did allow that even though Sam was meeting all the usual milestones, we should be prepared for anything.

We didn't know much about his birth parents beyond that they were young. But there was other stuff that worried me too. When Sam couldn't explain what he wanted, he'd run and hurl himself at doors. He didn't seem to have many fears or a natural sense of danger—he'd climb and jump off of everything and run with zero caution down the street. By bedtime my back ached from lunging after him and trying—and often failing—to keep him safe. He didn't follow instructions very well, or really at all. He was unusually tall for his age, and very adept at opening doors and unlocking child-proof gates. The director of his daycare wasn't successful at hiding her exasperation when she told us he was always sneaking out to explore other classrooms or to "help" the cook in the school's kitchen.

The spooky Greek Orthodox church, a hulking mountain of soot-darkened bricks in the middle of our residential block, should have been a warning sign. Sam's daycare was in its basement. The class had a small outdoor play area enclosed by a tall, wrought-iron fence—the kids looked like a Victorian zoo exhibit. One day at pickup, a caregiver pulled me aside to sign a form absolving them of responsibility because Sam had, in one of his bursts of puppyish energy, run straight into the fence, or maybe it was into another kid—the details were murky—and banged his mouth. Sam, holding my hand, looked up at me and grinned like it was the silliest story he'd ever heard. He seemed unfazed. But after a few days we could see that his two front teeth were wobbling and turning grey. A dentist recommended pulling them out. Sam would have a gap in his smile for at least four or five years, or whenever his permanent teeth arrived. The next month we switched him to another preschool with a bigger and softer play area.

I felt jealous of other parents with less challenging kids. On weekends I'd take Sam to Rainbow Songs, where moms and one or two dads sat with their toddlers in a circle while a caffeinated, peppy instructor with an acoustic guitar led us in a singalong. Sam wouldn't sit in my lap for more than a minute. Instead, he'd run and skip around the room, rooting through bags and knocking over the instructor's coffee. On the way home I'd see younger kids marching responsibly right beside mom or dad on the sidewalk, the parent absentmindedly scrolling through texts. Sam could never do that.

Those first years were tense. My jaw clenched tighter and tighter as Sam got more and more wild and unpredictable. I was ashamed at how much I looked forward to the moment when he would finally fall asleep at night. That's when the world was quiet and calm and so much easier. What I didn't want to admit was that there was something wrong with him. I told myself he was just one of those super-energetic kids and that maybe a switch would flick (at 4? at 5? at 16?) and he'd be "normal." One day he'd stop bolting into the street to jump in puddles, oblivious to us yelling for him to watch out for cars and get back on the sidewalk. He just needed to grow up.

Every day when I dropped Sam off at school or took him to the playground, I felt queasy watching him try to play with other kids. He was like an unpredictable dog let loose in the playground. Other kids instantly recognized that he was different. They paused and sometimes visibly recoiled. Then edged away or just ignored him. My Sam would look momentarily crushed, then move on.

Before he turned three, we took Sam to be assessed by a developmental pediatrician. The diagnosis: Sam was on the autism spectrum, a mild to moderate case. Although he was too young to assess for ADHD, that condition often goes hand in hand with autism, and he was showing all the signs.

It was like we'd become anthropologists tasked with trying to decode a person who was both familiar and alien. Sam was "verbal," meaning he'd made progress learning to express himself, unlike some autistic kids who never speak more than a few phrases. He "stimmed," meaning he'd make repetitive motor movements (mostly chewing on toys and rubbing our elbows and ears) when he needed some relief from sensory overload. Sometimes he "flapped" his hands in front of himself when he was stressed. He couldn't manage "transitions," meaning he'd go full nuclear meltdown if we tried to make him leave the park or do anything that wasn't on his living-in-the-moment itinerary.

I've lost track of how many occupational therapists, educational consultants, child psychologists, and behavioural analysts we've consulted. We took turns going to a night class for families with autistic kids. There were a dozen parents in the class, and we sat in a circle like we were in group therapy, which in a real sense we were. We wore name tags and sipped takeout coffees. The classes were supposed to supply us parents with strategies and make us feel less alone, but I'd leave every session feeling more anxious. One mom would try to hide her quiet sobbing from us each week. Near the end of the course, when it was her turn to share an update about how she was doing with her child, she broke down, trying to explain through tears that she spent every night worrying about what her daughter would never experience. Would she ever be able to have a career, fall in love, or have kids of her own? Another mom hugged her and reassured her that everything would be fine, that all of our kids would find some happiness. But all of us knew that wasn't always true.

One of the mysteries of autism is how some of the senses are in overdrive while others are more dulled than in the average person, and this mix-up of sensations profoundly impacts how the autistic person experiences the world around them. Some autistic kids are drawn to bright lights and shiny things, like moths to a flame, while others refuse to leave the house on a sunny day. Sam was especially sensitive to sound yet seemed to have little to no sense of how his body occupied space (which explained why he was always banging into fences and other kids). The sensations of eating were another challenge. I've met restaurant critics who pretentiously talk about the "mouthfeel" of a dish. But when it comes to a kid with autism, mouthfeel can be a make-or-break factor. Some autistic kids find comfort in one specific type of mouthfeel, perhaps the slithery-salty mouthfeel of SpaghettiOs, and refuse to eat anything else. Sam's hang-ups were less predictable. Some days he would decide that everything on the breakfast table was too spicy (even if the only spice involved was a little cracked pepper) and would eat only plain oatmeal. Other days, like Goldilocks, he would refuse to eat his oatmeal if it was too hot and then, five minutes later, decide it wasn't hot enough.

Then moments after he turned three, a breakthrough. Sam was running circles around our kitchen table, yipping and jumping, while I was pulling eggs out of the fridge. I hollered at him to be careful, and he kept running and yipping and jumping. I was about to yell again, but then saw how much fun he was having. I didn't want to stop his fun. I remembered the lessons from the autism parenting classes: I had to present him with something even more fun. So I pulled a stool up to the counter, pointed to it, and, in between his yips, asked Sam if he wanted to cook breakfast. He froze. He gave me a look that went, in a matter of seconds, from surprise to skepticism to pure glee. Yes, Dad!

I wasn't really going to let him cook breakfast—at least not by himself. We'd cook it together. Making breakfast together was weirdly easy. It turned out he loved to crack eggs. And he was really good—surprisingly better than me—at keeping bits of shell from breaking off into the bowl. Next I showed him how to mix those eggs with a whisk, pour out exact amounts of milk into measuring cups, and scoop out brown sugar (while taking a few spoonfuls for himself). All of a sudden he wasn't running in circles or hurling those same eggs across the room. He was proud to be helping and doing what Dad asked him to. See? he'd say with a huge smile and great pride. I did it!

We moved onto oatmeal and cream of wheat. Then omelettes with three cheeses, frittatas, shakshuka, and a fried egg sandwich. Not to mention crispy hash browns, piles of bacon, and farmer's sausage. And (this made someone else in the house very happy) lots and lots of French toast.

Start with a fun breakfast, and the rest of the day would be fun too.

A bonus was how making breakfast together encouraged Sam to talk. Instead of ignoring me, or demanding to watch videos on an iPad, he'd quiz me on why syrup is sticky. And why do we need to toast the Eggo instead of just eating it frozen? And why do we keep them in the freezer anyway? And what makes the freezer stay cold? So many questions!

I was proud of figuring out how to use our breakfast bonding time to get him to try stuff he'd otherwise refuse as too spicy or simply too weird. This was a way to sneak more vegetables into his diet. A few mushrooms in a cheese omelette. Shredded zucchini in a potato pancake. More shredded zucchini in a breakfast loaf.

Cooking together was also the golden ticket to building up his confidence, to working on his problem solving and his hand-eye coordination, and to keeping him focused on a series of tasks instead of flying off in a thousand distracted directions. Measuring amounts was a fun way to learn more about counting and simple math. Using a timer to tell us when something was ready helped him work on his patience and manage his emotions. The more we cooked together, the more I spotted how he approached each recipe like a science experiment, waiting to see what happened when one ingredient mixed with another, and what happened when it was heated or cooled.

Partly to answer Sam's morning interrogations, but also to satisfy my own curiosity, I spent evenings digging into the history and evolution of what we eat for breakfast and why. The stories behind many of the breakfast foods we unquestioningly cook every day can get very strange— for instance, how cereals like Corn Flakes were originally thought to keep people's minds away from temptations (masturbation, especially). Just as many dishes are rooted in special traditions or amazing aha moments. French toast isn't actually French, but was likely invented by the Romans—who, for the same reasons we make it today, saw it as a way to use up a less-than-fresh loaf of bread. Who had the smart idea to sprinkle their French toast with powdered sugar is another matter.

This book is a record of that first year of making every Sunday breakfast together with Sam. I had to keep our Sunday cooking time engaging for him and keep pushing beyond my usual breakfast repertoire. But I was also keeping breakfast interesting for myself. I'd travelled far from my monkish, mechanical mornings of a single slice of buttered toast. We were having fun cooking together, experimenting with new recipes and eating every last bite—even when breakfast was a flop. Sometimes we'd just make eggs plus toast with butter, and even though it was very similar to the buttered toast I used to make just for myself, it tasted so much better having made it together.

Most Sundays, Stephen was cooking with us, sharing in the fun and discovery. On those mornings when Sam and I planned to make an extra-big mess, with clouds of flour dusting the counters and a sink full of eggshells, we let him sleep in. Later he'd come downstairs to find our narrow kitchen table set for a big family meal. He'd even offer to help clean up.

The following chapters recap our morning adventures, revisit my own childhood obsessions, and go even further back to look at the origins of many of our favourite breakfast standards. I've included enough recipes to get you through 52 weekends, plus ideas for variations that'll carry you even further. The recipes are roughly ordered through our year, ranging from the simple but blissful Toast Soldiers (page 27) to my grandmother's more intricate kringel, a Christmas bread that'll require plenty of braiding practice (page 201). For Stephen, I included exactly four variations on French toast (pages 189, 194, 196, and 199).

Another bonus of our Sunday breakfast routine: it infiltrated the rest of the week. Like most households, we almost never have time to cook stuff from scratch Monday through Friday—not when the most urgent task is locating matching socks for school. But Sunday's happy halo made every breakfast feel a little more special. Even a bowl of supermarket cereal was an opportunity for us to grow as a family. Dad, Sam asked, do you hear my Rice Krispies singing?

Here and there in these recipes I've included tips on how to get that happy halo too. They worked for us and might for you. Here's an essential one: whether you're cooking breakfast for a kid, a partner, or for yourself, choose the right soundtrack. Around age two, Sam figured out how to twist the radio dial until he found a song he liked. Lately he's been obsessed with Fleetwood Mac's *Rumours*, which has got to be one of the bounciest breakup albums ever made. He'll boop-boop around the kitchen, swinging his arms through the air as Lindsey Buckingham encourages us to go our own way.

And we do.

EQUIPMENT

*What's in
My Kitchen*

My kitchen drawers are stuffed with multiple sizes of wooden spoons, spatulas, and whisks, not to mention a cherry pitter, an olive pitter, an avocado pitter (there is such a thing!), and a gadget that'll extract the seed from a mango (it leaves a mess). I've collected so many types of baking pans, hand mixers and stand mixers, mandoline slicers and spiralizers, cast-iron pots and fondue sets, that there's no way all of it would ever fit in our tiny kitchen. More than half of the stuff has been relegated to cupboards that stretch across the width of the basement, and now those cupboards are at capacity. I admit I have a weakness for kitchenware stores, where I always end up finding something I hadn't imagined a need for until that very moment. I'll sometimes fall asleep at night scrolling through stores' sites on my phone, and only remember that I bought something when the delivery courier shows up at our door. The problem with being known as someone with a lot of cookware is that it's inevitably what people give you as a gift too—so even if I've decided I have too much stuff, or try to purge some of it, the collection keeps growing.

But in my more rational moments, I'll admit, in a pinch, that I could get by with exactly eight kitchen basics, not a single special pitting device among them. Through trial and much error, I've got precise recommendations:

A silicone flipper. It's important that it's not plastic and never, ever metal, which will inevitably gouge your pans. The silicone should be semi-stiff—the flexible silicones seem to get more bendy with heat and time, and prove useless at flipping even something as light as a crêpe. I'm partial to a grey-blue model sold by Lee Valley that's just stiff enough and—a bonus—is one piece, which means the handle won't surprise you by popping off as you're attempting to fold an omelette. If you don't have a wooden spoon, or your spoon is already in use, this tool will just as easily help you scramble eggs. Plus, you can throw it straight into the dishwasher when you're done.

A medium-size whisk. In this case, always choose metal over silicone versions, which are too bendy to be of any use when whisking a thick batter or hand-whipping a bowl of cream to top your pancakes. I have a variety of sizes of whisks, but the one that gets the most use is the middle of the pack, which is just as good for blending a big bowl of pancake batter as it is for whipping a single egg white to a froth. The medium is also a good size for kids who take special pleasure in seeing how egg yolks blend into batter.

A 12-inch cast-iron skillet. I avoided cast-iron pans for too long. They seemed like a lot of work, between the regular seasoning of the surface and the fact that even the smallest ones weigh more than all your other pans combined. But the fact is that seasoning is very simple to do (just the occasional dab of oil rubbed into a warmed pan), they clean up ridiculously easily, and their solidity means they sear, fry, and cook everything very evenly. Unlike a non-stick pan, a cast-iron skillet will never betray you. It's surprise-free. It's the exact opposite of non-stick in that it gets better with use. And the more you use the pan, the more you'll want to use it. It'll become so familiar that it's like another member of the family. A big bonus: you can stick this pan in the oven, which means it can do double duty as a baking pan for upside-down cake or for those mornings when you crave a frittata. If you're investing in one, you might as well get a bigger one. A 12-inch skillet is a perfect size for cooking pretty much everything. It'll fit three or four smaller pancakes at a time, and there's enough space to fry eggs on one side and warm hash browns on the other.

A baking sheet. After a cast-iron skillet, this sheet will be your go-to cooking apparatus. I recommend a heavier, commercial-style sheet made of uncoated aluminum. The heavier-gauge sheets won't warp under heat (a common problem with the typical non-stick home-baker sheets). Look for a sheet with a raised rim (minimum of an inch). The rim has two uses: it allows you to bake mixes that start out wet (see Green Eggs and Ham, page 158) and it means that whatever you have baking on the sheet won't slide into the oven when you're pulling it out. You don't need to go to a restaurant supply store to find such sheets: sites like Amazon carry them for under $15.

Just one knife. Both home and professional cooks have many, many, MANY opinions about what knives you need for what purpose, but if pressed they'll all generally agree that all you really need is a single eight-inch chef's-style knife. And you don't need to spend a small fortune on it either. My J.A. Henckels knife was priced under $100, and I use it every day to do everything from peel an apple to slice through a bone-in chicken. The steel isn't as hard or light as some of the fancier Japanese options, but it's perfect for most home kitchen work and requires sharpening only a few times a year.

A large measuring cup. I'm talking about one of those eight-cup Pyrex models, or something similar. Make sure it has a spout. You need one this large mainly for batter-based breakfasts, as it allows you to mix your pancakes and easily pour them into the pan, all from the same bowl. It's also handy for mixing omelettes, dipping French toast, preparing easy muffin recipes . . . the list goes on. A plastic version might make more sense if you're worried about an overzealous kid whose mixing technique sometimes means the bowl ends up anywhere but on the kitchen counter. Parchment paper. Since I began making these big Sunday breakfasts with Sam, and generally spending more family time in the kitchen, I started to appreciate how it has a thousand uses. It's important for lining your baking sheet, but it also provides a handy counter surface cover if you're rolling out breakfast breads or mixing something especially messy (anything with flour or powdered sugar, for instance). It's also useful for making paper hats with your kid while you wait for the baking timer to go off.

A drip coffee maker. A turning point in our house was when I admitted that the pour-over coffee pot, for all its pros, had one massive con in that it required more time and alertness than I have first thing in the morning. That's when we hid it in the basement with the rest of our lesser-used kitchen gadgetry and pulled out our old Braun coffee maker with a thermos pot and an all-important timer. Now I grind beans and set the coffee maker the night before, then wake to its *I'm Ready!* beep. One less thing to think about.

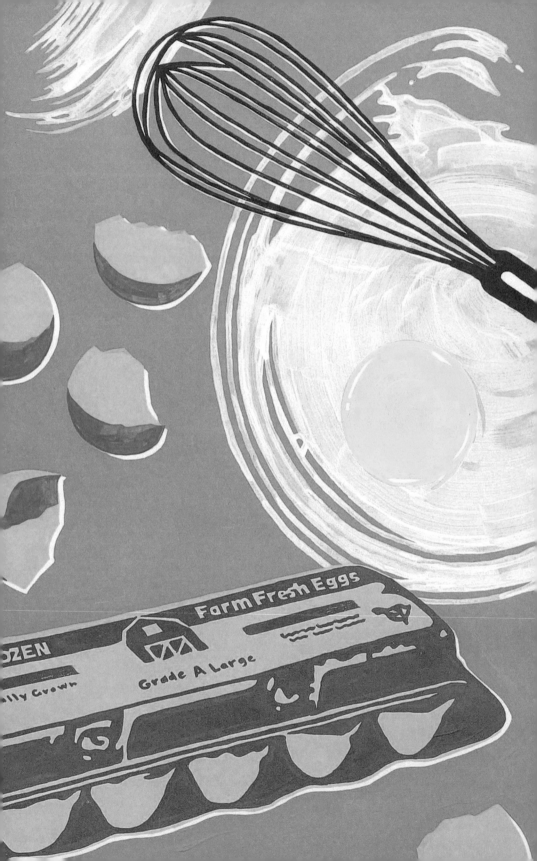

INGREDIENTS

A Few Essentials

Six in the morning isn't a time to be worrying about whether you have the exact right quantity of unsalted butter to bake a cake. If I don't, I'll risk the wrath of the baking gods and substitute salted, skip the amount of salt that a recipe calls for, and hope for the best. I designed the recipes in this book for the realities of home cooking—they aren't for a buttoned-down pastry chef. Replacing ingredients is something we all need to do sometimes, and I also suggest some easy alternatives. All that said, I use a shorthand in my ingredient lists, and there are often good reasons to use salted instead of unsalted butter—if you're frying eggs, for one, salted butter browns faster, giving the edges a crispy frill.

Here's a list of essential ingredients to cook the recipes in this book, with recommendations on alternatives:

Butter. Unless noted, this means salted. The salt in salted butter is a preservative, meaning it lasts longer than unsalted. It's still a good idea to look for the fresh, higher-fat butters from small producers rather than the industrial butters, which contain more water and are processed to have as long a shelf life as possible. Higher-fat, churned butters make toast tastier and produce better baked goods—the low water content creates flakier pastries and cooperates with baking powder to improve the rise of a cake.

Eggs, by which I always mean large eggs. I used to get medium-size, but once Sam came along, everything needed to be supersized. As with butter, the fresher the egg the better everything will taste. They don't need to be free-range, organic, or Omega-3 enriched, but it doesn't hurt. Out of habit I buy brown eggs, though there's no nutritional difference with a white egg (the chicken breed determines the shell colour). When I can I'll buy my eggs from the Amish farmer's stand at the weekly market in our neighbourhood park. Their shells are often mottled, brown, or even the pale blue of a winter sky. The yolks tend to be deep orange, nearly auburn, because the hens spend their days pecking grains and insects.

Flour. The default here is all-purpose. Some recipes will specify whole wheat flour, pastry flour, or a flour of ground nuts (I'm always sneaking ground almond flour into cakes for flavour and to help retain moisture). There's usually supermarket all-purpose in our cupboard for making pancakes or muffins. But if you can find flour ground from an independent mill, drop everything and buy a small bag. "Small" because it'll be pricey, but also because it usually grows stale faster than the highly processed supermarket versions. Fresh-ground flour almost always includes a label telling you exactly when it was ground—be sure to use it within a month of that date, ideally that same week. The flour from the independent mill will likely be ground from a heritage wheat—the couple of mills a day's drive from my house all seem to use Red Fife, which has a deeper, slightly nuttier flavour profile (if you're a fresh wheat fan, you find yourself obsessing about stuff like flavour profiles) than the average wheat flour. It's worth experimenting with a fresh-milled wheat for pie or tart crusts, pizza dough, or, really, any baked product for a special occasion. Every Sunday qualifies as a special occasion in my books.

Milk, meaning whole or 2% cow's milk. We often have non-dairy milks in our fridge (Sam is fond of unsweetened almond and oat milks on his cereal), but non-dairy varieties aren't one-to-one for cooking or baking.

Which is not to say they're impossible to cook or bake with. I'm partial to recipes, like Chocolate Rice Pudding (page 98), that use canned coconut milk, which can be as rich and sweet as condensed milk.

Pepper. Fresh-ground black pepper is best, but you can get away with pre-ground black pepper or even white pepper (though white tends to give more spice heat, so watch out if you've got a spice-phobic kid).

Salt. I use kosher or regular table salt in most recipes. Sometimes a fancy Maldon or flaked salt makes for a better final seasoning on top of an omelette or pizza.

Sugar. In most recipes that include sugar, I specify the granulated kind—also called regular or white sugar. It's white because the molasses has been refined out. It's also commonly called table or refined sugar, which for too long I misunderstood to mean that it was for polite company. At tea time. You can replace granulated sugar with a sweetener or other substitute, but the advantage of granulated-regular-white-table-refined sugar, especially for baking, is that it measures out easily and has the effect of aerating butter when they're beaten together (and so works as another leavening agent in your bake).

Vanilla. If you watched a lot of cooking shows in the 2000s, you'll be familiar with the moment in any baking recipe demonstration when the host (Nigella Lawson comes to mind) luxuriously scrapes the oozing, gunky brown pulp from a vanilla pod. But for the average home cook, vanilla pods are pricey and not always easy to track down. You could easily substitute vanilla extract. Or you can use vanilla paste, small jars of which are now carried in most supermarkets. Paste has nearly as intense a flavour punch as a fresh pod, and includes some of the characteristic flecks of vanilla seeds that you'd get from a pod too. It keeps forever in the fridge. Another advantage: you can substitute paste one-to-one for extract.

A Year of Sundays

THE RECIPES

SUNDAY

1

TOAST SOLDIERS

You can order toast soldiers for breakfast at the Greek diner around the corner, at a Four Seasons resort, and, really, anywhere they have eggs and bread on hand. But the best version is the one you make at home. Anyone who has had a kid, met a kid, or been a kid will know that toast soldiers are where it's at. The sliced-up toast is made for smaller hands and mouths. It also cools faster for kids who can't wait.

Toast soldiers were invented by the British, who'll gladly eat any and all toast, day and night. Why soldiers? Because the strips should be straight and narrow and toasted just enough to hold themselves upright—like a soldier guarding the palace of a sleeping queen. There's a theory that toast soldiers first became a breakfast staple because of a series of 1960s commercials made by the U.K.'s egg marketing board, starring a comedian named Tony Hancock—he was a household name for playing gullible characters on variety shows, that era's Steve Coogan. You can find these ads on YouTube, and they're worth watching (over breakfast) for a sense of how much and how little commercials have changed since the early years of TV.

In our house, Sam went through a months-long toast soldiers phase. We can vouch that the most versatile soldiers are made with store-bought sliced white bread, lightly buttered. Toasted white bread stands tall but will soak up everything you dunk it into, just like a sponge.

As recipes go, toast soldiers are the baseline for introducing your kid to the fun and surprises of cooking. There are even a few science lessons to impart, like why toasted bread is crisper (the toaster's heat evaporates the bread's water content) and why toasted bread is browned (that's the Maillard chemical reaction of heat combining the bread's outer layers of carbohydrates and amino acids). There's even a magic trick to ensuring that an egg's shell doesn't crack while it's boiling. For that, follow the steps below.

SERVES 2 TO 3

● ●

4 eggs

Salt and pepper to taste

4 slices bread

4 pats butter

● ●

Before we get to the cooking, there are two steps to prevent cracks forming on your eggs as they boil. First, don't put the eggs into the hot water straight from the fridge; let them come up to room temp. Second, there's a pocket of air inside every egg, which expands and causes the shell to crack as it heats. Using a pin, make a small hole in the blunt end of the egg before you place it in the water—this will help the heated air and steam get out.

Place the eggs in a medium saucepan and fill with enough water to just cover the eggs. Bring to a low boil, then reduce to a simmer. Simmer the eggs for a minute, then remove the saucepan from the heat and leave covered for 3 minutes. Any longer than that and the yolks will be too firm for the all-important dunking.

The moment you place the eggs in the saucepan, start toasting your bread. Butter the toasted bread, then slice into strips. Stack alternating strips (like Jenga pieces) on a plate for the centre of the table. If you have egg cups, serve the cooling eggs with the top quarter of the shell sliced off. Sprinkle with salt and pepper. If you don't have egg cups, you can substitute small juice glasses or, truthfully, just hold the egg upright on a plate with one hand. Then start dunking.

BANANA-KEFIR SMOOTHIES

Since the invention of the electric blender, people have been finding creative ways to ruin smoothies. At one end of the spectrum are the extreme health nuts who—like a former and not-missed housemate of mine—believe a true smoothie is thick with kale pulp and so tart from lemon juice that you can sip only a thimbleful at a time. At the other end are the people who prefer their smoothies to taste like a dessert, like the versions served at the kind of national coffee chain that makes them from ice, fruit-flavoured syrup, and full-fat milk. I'm somewhere in between—I want my smoothie to taste good, but not so good that I spend the rest of the day in a sugar coma.

Smoothies are so simple and fast to make—just dump what you have in the blender, and blend—that I hesitate to classify them as a Sunday breakfast. But once in a while we have a punishing Sunday schedule that allows us five minutes spent with the blender, then we're off. (On that note, those extra-large reusable cups with built-in lids and straws, the kind they seem to sell only at Starbucks and Winners, are exactly what you need for a to-go smoothie.)

An essential quality of a smoothie is that it's ice-cold, and to achieve that, many people will add ice cubes to the blend. But I find blended ice only ends up melting fast, diluting what nutritional advantages you're aspiring to, and hastening the smoothie's eventual separation. Instead of ice I use frozen berries, which means the smoothie will stay cold and keep its consistency much longer. I try to freeze as many bags of washed berries as I can during their peak seasons, but eventually you'll run out. Not to worry: grab a jumbo bag of frozen mixed berries next time you're at the supermarket. I always include a banana or two in the blend, and while some people like to use frozen bananas, the smoothie will be smoother and creamier if you opt for unfrozen. Because you're grinding up frozen fruit, it also helps if you have a blender with a tough motor. Super tough. I've busted a half-dozen blenders over the years making smoothies (frozen mango is especially punishing). If you add those dead blenders all up, it might justify shelling out for one of those restaurant-grade blenders, like a Vitamix. A couple of years ago I found a Vitamix knockoff that's yet to fail me. Fingers crossed.

The other big decision to make is your preferred liquid. Sometimes we'll use unsweetened almond milk, but I much prefer the sour edge of fresh kefir—that fermented milk drink that's related to yogurt but is much thinner and is said to have miraculous health benefits, like lowering cholesterol, managing blood sugar, and generally being all-around good for gut health. To balance out kefir's sourness, I'll add a couple of spoonfuls of peanut butter or whatever nut butter we have hanging around.

SERVES 2 TO 4

• •

2 to 2½ cups kefir or plain yogurt

2 cups frozen berries (a mix of whatever is in season or available)

1 cup frozen stone fruit or mango

2 bananas

2 spoonfuls peanut butter or other nut butter

1 spoonful honey

• •

Add all the ingredients to a blender and blend until smooth. If the mixture looks too thick, add more kefir. If it's too pulpy, add another banana and another tablespoon of nut butter and blend at a higher speed.

RICOTTA TOASTS

Not long ago, the entire world—or at the very least the world outside my door—went mad for toast. Every diner, coffee shop, and restaurant had to have a signature version. Toast with five kinds of mushrooms, toast with charred kale and sardines, toast with labneh and hazelnuts, and especially toast with avocado. It was like we'd all simultaneously figured out that toast is a blank canvas you can do pretty much anything with, and it'll taste great.

The toast trend can be credited, in part, to an L.A. cook named Jessica Koslow, who runs a mini empire centred on a breakfast spot, Sqirl. People line up before her doors open each morning, drawn by stories of the most amazing toast you've ever had. My favourite is always available, a slice of house-made brioche as thick as a novel, buttered and toasted on a pan, slathered from edge to edge with fresh ricotta, and finished with a couple of spoons of your choice of jam.

Every so often I get the urge to make that toast at home. If you have brioche, go for it. I'll usually opt for a thick slice of sourdough or pullman, which makes this recipe, for me, less like a dessert and more like a breakfast. Day-old bread is actually better than fresh from the bakery, as it'll toast up nicely and support heavier toppings. The combination of jam and fluffy cheese improves any slice.

Here I give instructions to make a quick jam, but the sky won't fall if you substitute store-bought, ideally from a small operation. Some days, I'll replace the jam with thin slices of fresh peaches, nectarines, or a tart apple—a Granny Smith or Mutsu—which nicely complement the cheese.

If you're out of ricotta, use a full-fat cream cheese. Just make sure it's the airy, whipped kind of cream cheese, not the thick version usually reserved for baking. A big part of the recipe's magic is the contrast of the fluffy cheese with the crunch of the toast. For Sam, it's watching the berries collapse into the cooking jam—and taking a spoon to the cooled pot.

SERVES 2

• •

2 cups raspberries

2 tablespoons lemon juice, divided

½ cup granulated sugar

1 tablespoon lemon zest

Pinch of salt

1 cup full-fat ricotta

2 tablespoons butter

4 slices day-old sourdough

• •

In a small pot, combine the berries, 1 tablespoon lemon juice, and the sugar. Stir over high heat until the sugar dissolves, the berries break down, and the mixture boils. Simmer for 10 minutes, smooshing the berries every once in a while with the back of a wooden spoon. If you're not a fan of raspberry seeds, strain through a fine-mesh sieve. Cool in a bowl at the back of the counter while you prepare the cheese and toast. (If you're thinking ahead, make the jam the night before and refrigerate.)

Preheat your oven broiler or toaster oven. Using a handheld electric mixer or a stand mixer with the whisk attachment, combine the remaining 1 tablespoon lemon juice, lemon zest, salt, and ricotta. Whisk on high until airy. (You could whisk by hand, but I recommend going electric to get maximum cloud-like volume in the cheese.) Set aside.

Butter both sides of the bread and toast under a broiler or in a toaster oven, turning once. You want it to be lightly charred but not blackened, which will take around 5 minutes. Spread the ricotta on the toast, then top with the cooled jam to taste.

FRIED EGG AND AVOCADO TOASTS

We all heard more than enough about avocado toast by the late 2010s, around the time someone started selling millennial-razzing T-shirts with the slogan "Let Them Eat Avocado Toast." (And while millennials might have popularized avocado toast, they didn't invent it.) There's a good reason avocado toast became so unavoidable. It's delicious, especially if you have freshly sliced rustic bread brushed with a bit of olive oil before going under a grill, then topped with slices of a perfectly ripe Hass avocado.

My own avocado toast addiction started with a university roommate named Catherine. This was the mid-1990s. We met while working on a campus paper and shared an apartment with two tiny bedrooms that could each just fit a twin-size bed (our working theory was that the apartment had previously been used as an acupuncture or massage clinic, and we slept in what had been treatment rooms). So we spent a lot of time studying for classes in the comparatively large kitchen, which was warmed by the afternoon sun. To keep us going, Catherine got into the habit of making lots and lots of snacks. Our go-to was avocado toast. We were lucky to be near an outdoor market with an endless supply of discounted bags of overripe fruit, and there was always a good chance of finding three or four soft but not-yet-browning avocados. We'd smear them on whatever was left in our bread box. At some point—we must have been preparing for exams—we stopped bothering to eat anything else. This went on for a month, and then, without discussing it, we just stopped. Too much of a good thing.

We certainly didn't invent avocado toast. That genius (someone in L.A. or Melbourne, I'd guess!) has been lost to time. The good news: avocado toast is rich in B vitamins and healthy monounsaturated fats. In India they call the avocado an alligator pear (for the bumpy skin) and a butter fruit (for the creamy insides). In California the avocado has long been worshipped for improving your skin, your sex drive, and your overall health. An avocado a day keeps the plastic surgeon away. They were originally cultivated in Mexico and Guatemala, though the most recognizable variety, the Hass, was patented in California in 1935 by a mailman and amateur horticulturalist named Rudolph Hass. He was looking to get rich, but other farmers ignored his patent and grafted their own Hass trees. At least he could point to his legacy: some 95 percent of the avocados grown in California, and many other parts of the world, are Hass.

Avocados are a gateway ingredient to get a kid to try many other types of food. Almost all kids are instant fans of guacamole, especially when it's fresh and creamy (no lumps!) and light on the lime juice. Add a few pieces of diced avocado to something—stewed goat tacos, baby kale salad, a BLT—and you're golden. But it took some gently persistent convincing to get Sam to agree that it belonged under a fried egg. When he finally gave in and took a bite, it was a happy shock. The combination of the creamy fruit and the crispy, frilly edge of the fried egg feels predestined and right—as inevitable a pairing as Ernie and Bert.

SERVES 2

• •

1 large ripe avocado (or 2 medium avocados)

Salt and pepper to taste

1 tablespoon olive oil

Butter, for frying

4 eggs

4 slices whole wheat bread

Sriracha (optional)

Small bunch cilantro, chopped (optional)

• •

In a small bowl, mash the avocado with a dash each of salt and pepper.

Fry the eggs—I prefer mine sunny-side up for this, but over easy is fine too. To get a crispy edge to your eggs, heat a skillet to medium-high, then add the oil and butter. Once the butter is spitting hot, crack the eggs into the skillet, then immediately lower the heat to medium. Remove the eggs when they've cooked to your preference.

Toast the bread while the eggs fry. Spread the mashed avocado on the toast, right up until the edge. Finish with a grind of pepper. Place a still-hot fried egg on top. If you (or a more adventurous kid) like extra heat, drizzle with sriracha. If I have some growing in the garden, I'll top it all with a few leaves of chopped cilantro.

SUNDAY

5

ALMOND BUTTER OVERNIGHT OATS

Sometimes—okay, very often—the last thing anyone wants after a week
of packing school lunches and folding a dozen loads of laundry and racing
through work deadlines and Zoom calls is to think about cooking. It's
those weekends when I feel least like cooking that Sam always wakes at
exactly six in the morning and zips around the house, singing at the top
of his lungs and pausing every minute to ask when we're getting up. The
singing turns into "I'm hungry-I'm hungry-I'm hungry."

Cleverer parents than me figured out a while ago that, barring a trip
to McDonald's, the easiest solution to the weekend breakfast challenge
is to prep breakfast the night before. Specifically, spend 5 minutes mixing
together some overnight oats. Oats have developed a reputation as
a superfood, and for good reason. They're gluten-free, high in fibre,
and crammed with vitamins and nutrients. Half a cup contains a good
fraction of your recommended daily intake of vitamins B1 and B5, zinc,
magnesium, and iron. But in my books they're also a superfood because
it takes little to no convincing for Sam to eat them. And making them the
night before is something like a magic trick. Plus, you can mix just about

anything with them as an add-in, especially yogurts, nut butters, preserves, and diced fresh fruit, and the textures meld together easily. The proportion of wet ingredients to dry matters, but beyond that it's hard to go wrong, and—bonus—it's one of those dump-and-stir recipes that are good for safely involving young kids in making.

The next morning, you can serve the oatmeal cold from the fridge or warm it in the microwave for a minute if someone prefers it hot, which we totally do. Hot oatmeal is the breakfast equivalent of a warm, fuzzy blanket. It's instant coziness, and instantly comforting, especially after one of those weeks.

SERVES 1

• •

½ cup rolled oats

½ cup milk or non-dairy substitute

½ tablespoon chia seeds

Spoonful of almond or other nut butter

Optional add-ins

Spoonful of fruit jam or marmalade

Pinch of cinnamon or nutmeg

Dried fruit like raisins, apricots, or cranberries

Berries, diced stone fruit, sliced mango, or sliced banana

Chopped peanuts, almonds, or pecans

Drizzle of honey or sprinkle of brown sugar

Chocolate chips

• •

In a 2-cup jar or large coffee mug, mix together the oats, milk, chia seeds, and nut butter until combined. Cover with plastic wrap and stick in the fridge overnight (this can be prepared 2 or 3 days ahead).

Where this recipe gets interesting is what you decide to add to it, either for the overnight soak or as a next-day topping. Overnight, that could be a spoonful of jam, spices like cinnamon or nutmeg, or dried fruit. For the next day, I like to set up the breakfast equivalent of a make-your-own-sundae bar. Whatever you have on hand, aim for a range of healthy (sliced bananas, blueberries, nuts, honey) to less healthy but no less essential (brown sugar, chocolate chips, more jam).

Note: This recipe is designed for one but can easily be multiplied by how many people you want to feed. I recommend including a spoon of almond butter, which I find adds sweetness and heft to oatmeal. Other nut butters will do fine, though some (especially peanut butter) can overpower the oatmeal flavour and turn your breakfast into something more like a Reese's cup.

SUNDAY

6

BREAKFAST PIZZA

At least once a month, I'll play a game with Sam in which we try to guess what each other wants for breakfast. I know what his answer is (it's always the same), but I'll instead guess increasingly ridiculous things (artichoke pancakes? porcupine pie? alligator soup?), which sends him rolling and giggling on the floor. The actual answer: pizza. Like a pair of frat boys, we'll happily have leftover pizza for breakfast. But making a breakfast pizza is even more fun, between rolling the dough and spreading out the toppings, half of which seem to disappear into our mouths before they make it onto the pizza and into the oven.

We've breakfast-ified our pizza by swapping in chèvre for mozzarella and bacon for pepperoni. The roasted squash is an extra step, but it's good for you, and besides, you need to preheat the oven anyway. If I'm planning ahead, I'll make my own dough (it's easy, as long as you have all-purpose flour and dried yeast, plus a few hours to let it rise), and if I'm really ambitious I'll make extra to freeze for another day. But most supermarkets now carry premade pizza dough, fresh or frozen, and if you're really stuck you can even swap in some store-bought puff pastry—which will make the pizza more of a tart, but who's complaining?

SERVES 4

· ·

2 tablespoons coarse cornmeal

1 butternut squash, peeled, seeded, and chopped into ½-inch cubes

2 tablespoons olive oil, plus more for brushing on the dough

6 slices bacon, chopped into 1-inch pieces

1 package (1 pound) fresh pizza dough (see note)

1½ cups crumbled semi-firm chèvre

· ·

Preheat the oven to 425°F. Lightly cover two baking sheets with cornmeal.

Toss the cubed squash in the olive oil, spread in a single layer on a parchment-lined baking sheet, and roast for a good half hour or until the pieces are easily poked through with a fork and slightly caramelized.

While the squash is baking, heat a skillet to medium-high and fry the bacon until the fat is rendered. Remove from the heat just before it starts to crisp up, and set aside on a sheet of paper towel.

Now it's time to form the dough. Divide the ball of pizza dough into two. There should be enough to cover two conventional-size rectangular baking sheets (but you can divide the dough further, if you choose, and make personal pizzas). Rub some olive oil on your hands and on a clean counter surface. Working with one ball at a time, spread the dough out using the heel of your hand. After a minute the dough will become stretchier and spread more easily—you want to get it to ⅛ inch thick. Using the back of both hands, lift the dough onto one of the prepared baking sheets that's been lightly covered with cornmeal, and stretch to meet the edges (trying to avoid tearing the dough). I find pizza dough incredibly unpredictable (depending on the humidity and how long it's been sitting out), but as is true of most things, it becomes easier to handle with practice. Cover the finished dough with parchment paper and repeat with the second.

Once both pies are formed, remove the paper and layer on your toppings. I start with the squash, dot the cheese in between, and end with the bacon. Finish by brushing the edges of each pizza with olive oil. They should take 10 to 15 minutes to bake and are done once the edges are browned, the bacon is crisp, and you can slide a spatula under the pizza and it lifts easily from the sheet.

If you have leftovers (you won't!), store in the fridge in an airtight container. They'll keep for a day. Reheat on a baking sheet for 15 minutes in a 250°F oven.

Note: An hour before you plan to make the pizza, take the dough out of the fridge and let it come to room temperature in a bowl that you've brushed with olive oil; cover the bowl with a damp tea towel.

SUNDAY

7

CRÊPES STACK

When I was growing up, we had one sacred morning rule: no talking to Mom before her coffee. On rare weekends we'd find Mom already caffeinated, humming along to the radio, and making crêpes. I'd double-check: was it someone's birthday? I loved crêpes more than anything. I'd pile my plate with them, along with strawberries and maple syrup and clouds of whipped cream.

Mom used a dead simple recipe from the *Joy of Cooking*, doubled: one cup of flour, one cup of milk, half a cup of room-temp water, some sugar and salt, half a stick of melted butter, and four large eggs. But as with all simple recipes, there was a trick: if you mixed the batter the night before and left it to froth and settle in the fridge, the crêpes would turn out thinner and lighter, with lacy edges.

One day when I was 10 or 11, she showed me how to pour the batter into the pan and then twist the pan around so the crêpe spread out as thin as the batter would allow. The twist was harder than it looked, but soon I figured it out. (It helps to use a lighter pan, is one secret.) That lesson was like a switch flicked. From that moment, I was in charge of my breakfast destiny.

Now I'm the parent who can't function without that first coffee. After a few sips I'm ready to cook anything, even tricky crêpes. Sam, like any reasonable kid, is a big fan. We share a fascination with how bubbly and full the batter looks when you pull it out in the morning. And we both live for the superthin, crispy, lacy edges of a perfectly cooked crêpe. Pretty soon, I'll teach him the twist.

The one drawback about making crêpes is that I can never make them fast enough to keep everyone happy. Unless you have multiple pans going, you'll be stuck at the pace of making one thin crêpe at a time—which is not going to fly when you have hungry kids or, worse, another hungry dad at the table. One solution is to get up earlier than everyone else and start flipping through crêpes, keeping the stack warm in the oven. But if you leave them warming too long, that stack will stick together and be about as easy to pull apart as a hockey puck. My solution is to borrow a page from the French patisserie dessert and assemble a cake of crêpes and cream.

Often called a mille crêpe cake (meaning a thousand crêpes), the basic idea is to create a tower of crêpes, with each layer separated by a thin layer of whipped cream. Before you stack the next crêpe, it must be mostly cooled, or else the heat will make the whipped cream melt out. If you're doing it right, there should be a thin, visible layer separating each crêpe—it's no hockey puck. My preferred variation is to combine whipped cream with mascarpone cheese, which builds the creaminess of the cake and keeps it from being too sweet. To serve, slice the cake into wedges as you would a typical cake.

SERVES 4

• •

1 cup all-purpose flour

3 tablespoons granulated sugar

1 teaspoon salt, divided

4 eggs

1 cup milk

½ cup water

4 tablespoons melted unsalted butter

Butter, for frying

2 cups whipping cream

¾ cup mascarpone cheese, at room temperature

2 tablespoons powdered sugar, plus more for dusting the finished cake

1 teaspoon lemon zest

• •

In a large bowl, combine the flour, sugar, and a pinch of salt. In a separate bowl, whisk the eggs, milk, water, and melted butter. Pour the wet ingredients into the dry and whisk until smooth. Cover the bowl and leave in the fridge overnight.

Melt the butter in a medium skillet on medium heat. Give the batter one more brief whisk to ensure it's fully combined, then pour ¼ cup onto the skillet, giving the pan a twist so it spreads in a thin, even layer. If you have two pans available, you could cut your time in half by frying crêpes in both pans at once. A crêpe is ready to flip when small bubbles appear and the surface appears drier, usually within a minute. To flip, gently slip a thin, wide spatula under the crêpe, working your way around to make sure no sections are sticking to the pan, and then in one swift move lift it a good 6 inches above the pan and then flip. The crêpe is fully cooked when the edges are crisp. Repeat this process (you should get about 24 crêpes out of this batter). Whatever you do, don't stack the crêpes together before the assembly stage—they'll stick into one big lump. Instead, separate each completed crêpe with a sheet of parchment paper, or if you have a lot of counter space, spread them out on one long sheet of parchment.

In a large bowl, whip the cream, mascarpone, powdered sugar, lemon zest, and remaining salt until it forms soft peaks. When the crêpes are cooled, stack them one by one on a serving plate, spreading a scant ¼ cup of the cream evenly across the crêpe with a spatula. Repeat this process until you've finished the layering of crêpes and cream spread. The finished stack should be served at room temp. Just before serving, dust it with some powdered sugar.

EASTER EGGS AND MUSHROOM TOASTS

In the days before Easter, the only conversation in our house concerns how many chocolate eggs the bunny will leave. But for a few hours, we'll busy ourselves with eggs of a non-chocolate type. Once we could trust Sam around a boiling pot of water, I got him involved in dyeing eggs just like his great-grandma does, using a natural colouring source: onion skins. The finished eggs are decorative and edible—our annual Easter Sunday breakfast.

Dyeing eggs with papery onion skins is the old-timey method in parts of Europe, especially in Greek Orthodox communities. I use yellow onions, which turn the eggshells shades of orange and brown, but you can also try red, which leaves them a greenish hue. The simplest route is to stick your eggs and skins loose in a pot of water and boil them together for 5 minutes. For more interesting effects, you'll need cheesecloth or sections of a nylon stocking (the latter is easier to work with) and a handful of rubber bands. With those, you can wrap the skins directly over the egg and then wrap cheesecloth on top—this will create a mottled effect. The third option is to place herb leaves or flowers on the eggs, then wrap them tightly in cloth and boil them for five minutes—the plants will leave a silhouette pattern on the eggs. Whichever option you choose, once you remove the pot from the heat, leave the eggs to soak for a further 15 minutes to get the full effect of the dye. A bonus: unlike store-bought pastel-coloured dyes, the onion dye on a dried egg won't transfer onto every surface it touches.

Another thing you can do with boiled eggs that you can't with chocolate ones is play a game of egg tapping. In our family, that means each person at the table chooses a dyed egg as their weapon. Holding an egg tightly in your hand, you tap your opponent's egg. The person whose egg cracks first gets cut from the bracket. And the person whose egg survives every round wins. What do they win? A chocolate egg, of course.

At the end of the game there's a lot of boiled eggs to eat. To round out the breakfast menu, I like to make hot mushroom toasts, which are loaded with herbs and butter and just as delicious on their own.

SERVES 4

· ·

For the eggs

6 to 8 onions (a mix of yellow and red)

1 dozen eggs

Leafy herbs or flowers for decoration (optional)

For the toasts

2 tablespoons olive oil

1 tablespoon unsalted butter

1 pound mushrooms (button, shimeji, or a mix)

1 clove garlic, crushed

Salt and pepper to taste

2 teaspoons lemon juice

Small bunch Italian parsley, chopped

1 tablespoon fresh thyme leaves

¾ cup whipped cream cheese

4 to 6 thick slices toasted rye or seeded bread

· ·

⟶

Peel the yellow and red skins of the onions, reserving the onions themselves for a soup or another recipe. Wrap the eggs in the onion skins and then in cheesecloth or a nylon stocking, and secure each with a rubber band. Cover with water in a large pot. Bring to a boil and let them cook for a further 5 minutes, then remove the pot from the heat and let stand for an additional 15 minutes. Alternatively, if you're decorating the eggs with herbs and flowers, place one or two stems on each egg, wrap with the cheesecloth, submerge into a pot of water with loose onion skins, then boil for 5 minutes and let stand for 15.

Remove the eggs from the water with a slotted spoon and let cool completely before unwrapping the eggs. To give them time to cool, and because the onion-wrapping process is somewhat finicky for first thing in the morning, it's best to make the eggs at least a day ahead. They can be stored for up to 4 days, uncovered, in the fridge.

Make the mushrooms the morning you plan to serve this dish. In a skillet on medium heat, warm the oil and butter, then add the mushrooms, garlic, salt, and pepper and slowly fry until they soften and begin to caramelize. Add the lemon juice, parsley, and thyme. Stir to combine until the herbs are just wilted. Set aside.

Spread the cream cheese on the toasted bread, then spoon on the mushroom mixture. Depending on the size of your slices of bread, you might want to slice them in half—a bite can get messy. Serve the dyed eggs alongside the toast.

A BAGEL BAR

Say you grew up in a small city any time before the 1990s. Say you were addicted to *Seinfeld* and Nancy Meyers movies. If that was you, you spent your days asking why it was so impossible to find a decent bagel. Or find any bagel, period. Bagels were mystical objects—they were what the people on TV and in movies took for granted. Did you, once you were college age, move to the biggest city you could find just to be closer to bagels? Maybe you did. Who can blame you?

Today bagels are on the shelves of the remotest 7-Eleven, but we're not necessarily better off. Most of those bagels don't come close to the real thing—they're just round discs of bread with holes drilled through the middle. They stay suspiciously fresh a week or more, when a true bagel, as any bagel addict knows, isn't much good half a day after it was baked.

I've ruined a few dinner parties by expatiating about which city, and which bagelry in that city, makes the absolute best bagels. Personal bagel loyalties have everything to do with which baker you feel closer to—physically and spiritually. There may now be bakers wood-firing very good bagels in California and Texas, even in the middle of Alaska. But you can't tell that to anyone from New York or Montreal. Each of those two bagel cities has its own specific bagel tradition and lore.

Like pretty much everything from New York, its bagels are bigger and certainly more famous. If they're baked right, the crust crackles while the insides remain dense and chewy, the better to slice and layer with an inch of cream cheese plus capers and lox, or to make an egg salad sandwich. Montreal's version is denser, flatter, and slightly sweeter because they're briefly boiled in honey-infused water before they're baked in wood-fired ovens. Leonard Cohen was said to live on them. Montreal's bakers claim their version is closer to the Ashkenazi original, as it debuted in Poland way back in the 15th century.

For a while I was a New York–style guy. I'd start most mornings with a sesame bagel. In Toronto I'd get my New York–style bagels from a place named Gryfe's, which has been in business since 1915 and hasn't changed how they hand-form each bagel. It had recently been run by the founder's great-grandson, Moishe Gryfe, until he passed away in 2021.

Then I moved to Montreal and my old fixation crumbled like so many bagel chips. My apartment was a short hike from the city's two most famous bagel shops: Fairmount (opened 1919) and St-Viateur (the youngster, from 1957). Everyone in Montreal—and I mean *everyone*, it's practically a municipal bylaw—starts the day with a bagel. They also tend to end the day with one, especially if they want to avoid a hangover (last call isn't strictly observed there). Both Fairmount and St-Viateur are open round-the-clock—or, more precisely, their front doors are always open, even on the coldest winter nights, to let out steam.

Montreal bagels are best in those first minutes after they've been pulled from the oven. That's when you get the full effect of the malty, honey-sweetened dough, the nuttiness of toasted sesame, and the trace of char and applewood smoke from the crackling wood-burning oven.

While I still love New York–style bagels, I now think of them principally as conduits for cream cheese and lox and whatever else I'm in the mood for—they're the base (a great base!) for a sandwich.

Montreal bagels, on the other hand, I'll eat on their own, no butter or cream cheese or anything, especially when they're still warm. Toppings would get in the way.

"Bagel" was one of Sam's first words. Or rather, he'd demand "bakels." When he was teething, we'd hand him a frozen bagel. After those teeth finally came in, we'd carry baggies of bagels around with us wherever we went, for when he demanded a snack.

Bagels are also the easiest way to impress overnight houseguests at breakfast time. I sneak out of the house at daybreak and pick up a dozen fresh bagels: poppyseed, sesame, and all-dressed. At our kitchen table, I set up a make-your-own-bagel bar, with the bagels stacked in a couple of precarious towers on a square plate—an approximation of the way that some bagel bakeries cool their bagels stacked up on wooden poles. To round out the meal, I'll provide some fruit and a couple cartons of juice. But the only thing anyone seems to care about is getting to the toaster first.

SERVES AS MANY AS YOU LIKE

• • • • • • • • • • • • • • • • • • • •

Savoury

Whipped cream cheese

Smoked salmon (wild B.C. is best)

Capers

Finely sliced red onions (if you have time, quick-pickled in red wine vinegar)

Gherkins, plus more for snacking

Other pickled veg (a mild, mixed giardiniera is my go-to)

Fresh dill

Sweet

Assortment of jams and jellies

Nut butter

Chocolate-hazelnut spread (why not?)

Sliced bananas

Salted butter

• • • • • • • • • • • • • • • • • • • •

⟶

This isn't so much a recipe as some ideas for how to prep a first-rate make-your-own-bagel bar. To be safe, assume you'll need two bagels per person. If a lot of people want them toasted all at once, it can be easier to place sliced bagels on a baking sheet and toast them in the oven.

For toppings, divide your bagel bar into savoury and sweet sides. Quantities depend on what you know about your guests' preferences. It's a good idea to buy more than you need, put out half the quantity, and pull out the rest when the first batch starts to disappear.

ONE-PAN EGGS AND CHORIZO

The tale of the princess and the pea doesn't seem that far-fetched if you've met a young kid. Sam can detect the tiniest fleck of scallion in a stir-fry. He'll fight another forkful: "It's yuck." Other days, he's on the lookout for anything that's too spicy, and imitates a fire truck siren if he sees my hand reaching for the peppermill. But I found a loophole: he'll eat anything if there's sausage involved, even if the sausage is mildly spicy or flavoured with herbs. It's not a great idea to be stuffing your kid with processed meats all the time, but there's less of a health risk with fresh and organic sausages, especially if they're prepared by a butcher you know. Fresh chorizo can be especially delicious at breakfast, and I usually get a milder version, which will still give a spicy heat. This recipe is something of a lazy-morning frittata. It involves a certain amount of prep (slicing potatoes, mainly), but it's otherwise easy and fast, and while the sausage is browning you can brew coffee and get other stuff done. The smoked paprika in the chorizo will colour everything else a brilliant sunset red.

SERVES 4

• •

2 tablespoons olive oil, divided

1 medium yellow onion, thinly sliced

1 teaspoon salt

10 ounces white mini potatoes

1 pound fresh chorizo

6 eggs

• •

Preheat the oven to 375°F.

Add 1 tablespoon oil to a large skillet set to medium heat. Once hot, start frying the onions. I usually sprinkle them with salt, which helps the onions' liquids release and prevents them from browning too fast. Meanwhile, slice the mini potatoes into quarters and add them to the pan along with the remaining 1 tablespoon oil. Stir every so often for 10 minutes, but not too much (you want the onions and potatoes to brown).

While the onions and potatoes are browning, remove the sausage from its casings and break into bite-size chunks. Once the potatoes have softened, add the sausage and, stirring occasionally, let it brown. This will take 5 to 10 minutes.

Once the sausage appears cooked through, create six divots between the sausage and potatoes. Crack an egg into each divot. Transfer the skillet to the oven and bake for 10 minutes or until the whites of the eggs are set. Slice into wedges and serve.

APPLESAUCE STREUSEL MUFFINS

I thought I knew the difference between cupcakes and muffins. Then
Sam asked me why I was calling his cupcakes that we'd made for breakfast
"muffins." Was it because they didn't have icing? He loved cupcakes. He
wasn't so sure if a muffin was something to get excited about. I started to
explain that cupcakes are more like cake while muffins are . . . um, well,
hmmm. He was right: most muffins are sweet enough to be mistaken for
cupcakes. And most cupcakes are the same dimensions as a muffin,
except for when they come from a bakery or kitchen where the cupcake
maker tops each one with a hat of swirling icing.

Cupcakes and American-style muffins (to distinguish them from
English muffins, or quick flatbreads) both debuted around the same time,
in the early 1800s. Back then they were easier to tell apart. The former
uses a cake batter, while the latter is more strictly a quick bread and in its
earliest incarnations was plainer and more wholesome than today's sweet
muffins. The origin of the name "cupcakes" is right in front of our faces:
they are simple cakes whose ingredients are measured out using cups
rather than by weight (whereas a pound cake uses a weight measurement).

Cupcakes were served as a dessert, often to kids, while muffins were a snack to get you through the day. Because muffins often get made with a certain amount of oats or hearty flours, and can sometimes contain shredded zucchini or carrot, they have the reputation for being good for you, or at least healthier than cupcakes. But they often contain as much sugar and fat as a cupcake. I'm firmly of the opinion that any muffin that tastes too good for you probably isn't worth eating. Muffins should be sweet—a treat. If they aren't, you should just be eating a slice of seven-grain bread.

My firm opinions about what makes a good muffin formed in the 1980s in the mall. Many Canadian malls had a store that sold only muffins, under the amazing name Mmmuffins. (Its actual name was Marvellous Mmmuffins, but the "marvellous" felt redundant and everyone just called it by its shorthand name.) That store's innovation was to make gigantic muffins (maybe that's why it needed so many extra letters in its name?), which were mostly muffin top, always very moist, and in many respects more like a cake. My recipe here is an attempt to recreate my favourite Mmmuffin muffin. You can use chopped apples instead of applesauce, but I find the applesauce helps keep them moist—and, anyway, not all kids are fond of chunks of apple in their muffins.

MAKES 2 DOZEN MUFFINS

· ·

1½ cups all-purpose flour, divided

1 cup whole wheat flour

1 cup quick-cook steel-cut oats

2 tablespoons baking powder

2 teaspoons cinnamon, divided

1 teaspoon salt

½ teaspoon nutmeg

2 eggs

1¼ cups packed brown sugar, divided

½ cup vegetable oil

½ cup milk

1½ cups applesauce

¼ cup butter, diced

1 tablespoon water

1 cup chopped pecans

· ·

Preheat the oven to 375°F. Grease two 12-cup muffin tins and dust with flour (or use muffin cup liners).

In a large mixing bowl, combine 1 cup all-purpose flour, whole wheat flour, and oats. Add the baking powder, 1 teaspoon cinnamon, salt, and nutmeg and mix well. In a separate large mixing bowl, whisk together the eggs, 1 cup sugar, oil, milk, and applesauce until smooth. Mix together the wet and dry ingredients until just combined, and set aside.

To make the streusel topping, combine the remaining ½ cup all-purpose flour, 1 teaspoon cinnamon, and ¼ cup sugar in a small bowl. Add the butter and water to the dry ingredients. Using your fingers (kid activity!), rub the butter into the dry ingredients until it forms a crumbly mixture. Lastly, add the pecans.

Spoon the muffin batter into the prepared muffin tins. Top each with a spoonful of the streusel. Bake for 20 to 25 minutes, until a toothpick inserted into a muffin comes out clean.

You can store these in an airtight container for 3 days. They also freeze well for a couple of weeks—just pop one in a toaster oven for 5 minutes to warm it up.

PLANTAIN FRITTERS

Like all new parents, we didn't much leave the house in those first few months with Sam. Opening the front door meant a lot of prep and psyching ourselves up. Packing and repacking the baby bag with diapers and snacks and distracting toys. Timing an outing exactly right so we didn't bump up against his naps and cranky episodes. And doing our best to look like we knew what we were doing—that these two gay dads had it figured out.

Then the cabin fever set in, and we agreed that we had to try doing some of the stuff we used to do pre-Sam, like restaurants. That's when we realized we weren't the only parents with a baby trying to go out, or even the only gay dads. Their kids were loud too, and they also took up extra space with high chairs blocking restaurant aisles and fold-up strollers poorly hidden in a corner. The reason we hadn't seen any of those families before is because they all went out to eat just when many places open for dinner service, when the dining rooms are emptier. We became part of the five o'clock crew.

In those first idyllic years before Sam figured out how to unbuckle his high chair and run around the tables, we took him to all our usual places.

He'd try everything at least once. We found out he had some expensive tastes (he gobbled up foie gras and pasta blanketed in truffled shavings). Our favourite any-day-of-the-week spot was La Cubana, a restaurant owned by a Toronto chef who'd recreated her dad's Havana diner, right down to the pistachio-green walls and the recipe for a plate of molasses-roasted pork with rice and beans. We always asked for the tostones—green plantain that's been sliced, pressed, and fried twice, like hefty potato chips with a chewy centre. Sam would commandeer most of them, as well as most of our rice and beans and a good portion of our molasses pork.

Tostones are nice any time of day, but even better for breakfast are plantain fritters, which are very similar, though more common a few islands over, in Jamaica. The main difference is that the plantains aren't used raw but are ripened for up to two weeks, until their skins are almost entirely black, so they can be mashed. If you don't have plantain, you can make the fritters with ripe bananas. But the starches in plantain make for a better fritter. Plus, they're much more filling than bananas, which is always a prime objective with kids. They're so filling, you could get away with a breakfast of just fritters, but we usually will scramble some eggs too, or we'll make a smoothie if we have a lot of other ripe fruit hanging around. The creamy eggs or smoothie pairs well with the hot and lightly spiced fritters. Preparing the batter is an ideal kid activity, especially if you have a kid who loves to help mash.

SERVES 4

• •

2 ripe plantains or 4 ripe
    bananas
1 cup all-purpose flour
2 tablespoons granulated sugar
1 teaspoon salt

½ teaspoon vanilla paste
½ teaspoon cinnamon
½ teaspoon nutmeg
½ cup vegetable oil

• •

Peel and slice the plantains, then mash them in a mixing bowl until you have a smooth pulp. Mix in the flour and sugar, and then the salt, vanilla, cinnamon, and nutmeg. You should have a sticky batter.

In a cast-iron skillet over medium heat, heat the oil. In batches, spoon the batter into the pan like you would with pancakes, ¼ cup per fritter. Turn down the heat to medium-low. Once the fritter starts to firm up, flip with a spatula. Use your spatula to press down each fritter so there's more surface area. They're done when both sides are well browned, about 10 minutes. As you work on the next batch, keep the cooked fritters warm on a plate loosely covered with paper towel and, over that, a clean tea towel. Serve warm.

If you have any left over, it's best to keep them at room temperature and have them as a midmorning snack. Like pancakes, they lose their crispiness when refrigerated and reheated.

ZUCCHINI QUICHE AND FARMER'S SAUSAGE

I made a point of showing Sam each step of making a quiche because it was one of the first recipes my mom helped me master. It was during summer break from school and the *Toronto Star* was running a weekly series of cooking-is-fun-for-kids recipes. I had nailed a recipe for a basic ratatouille, but failed at quiche week. The crust was impossible. So my mom stepped in and steered me away from the newspaper recipe (who wrote those, anyway?) and toward her James Beard cookbooks, which had very wordy instructions that weren't any easier to pull off than what was in the paper. We gave up on that, and Mom returned from the store with a frozen Tenderflake crust, into which we dumped the quiche's mixed eggs and cheeses and herbs. Into the oven it went. I'd made a quiche! A cheat's quiche, but still a quiche.

The secret about quiche is that once you know the basic principles, you don't really need a recipe. It's one of the easiest versions of a pie to make, which makes me wonder why it was a focus of such intense 1980s fascination. Today my favourite quiche inspiration comes from those 1980s cookbook icons, Julee Rosso and Sheila Lukins. What they call springtime quiche is really an excuse to eat a cup of grated cheese (they use Monterey Jack, another 1980s obsession). The "springtime" comes from the addition of fresh herbs, chopped tomatoes, and spinach. Depending on the herbs you use, it can have a pizza-esque flavour profile (always a plus with kids). It's also one good way to sneak green vegetables into Sam's diet. My version swaps out the spinach and tomatoes for zucchini and leeks. The other big reason we love this recipe so much: it's crustless. The quiche bakes in a buttered pie plate and forms its own crispy edge. No need to roll dough or even resort to a store-bought frozen shell.

I always serve slices of the cooling quiche with small farmer's sausages, which you can bake in the same oven.

SERVES 4

• •

8 farmer's sausages (look for the stubby, breakfast-size kind)

2 tablespoons olive oil, divided

2 medium zucchini (ideally one green and one yellow), diced

1 leek, green parts discarded and white section sliced into thin rounds

1 cup milk

4 eggs

1 cup grated mild cheese (Monterey Jack or a mild cheddar)

¼ cup freshly grated parmesan

¼ cup chopped Italian parsley

2 teaspoons lemon zest

Pepper, to taste

1 tablespoon panko bread crumbs

• •

Preheat the oven to 350°F. Butter the base and sides of a 9-inch
pie plate.

Arrange the sausages in an 8-inch stoneware baking dish with
1 tablespoon olive oil. Place on the middle rack of the oven for
30 to 40 minutes, until browned.

While the sausages bake, heat a cast-iron skillet to medium with the
remaining 1 tablespoon olive oil. Fry the zucchini and leeks until
the leeks are translucent and the zucchini is soft but not collapsing,
about 8 to 10 minutes. Place in a bowl and let cool on the counter.

In a medium-size mixing bowl, combine the milk, eggs, mild cheese,
parmesan, parsley, lemon zest, and pepper. Stir in the cooled vegetables
until evenly distributed.

Pour the quiche mix into the pie plate and sprinkle with the bread
crumbs and more fresh-ground pepper. Bake beside the sausages
on the middle rack for about 30 minutes, until the top is starting
to brown. Serve warm. If you have any left over, it'll make for a nice
midafternoon snack.

SUNDAY

14

PARMESAN SHIRRED EGGS
AND FLAT BACON

In our house we use parmesan more than salt. Come to think of it, we
often use it instead of salt to season salads, steamed veggies, baked
potatoes, pastas, polenta, and especially our eggs. The small wedges at
the grocer only get us so far in a month, so instead we get chunky sections
from a wheel. Since we're using it so often, I usually buy a younger, less
expensive grade of parmesan—we'll only get the dry, exquisitely nutty
stuff that's been aged four years or more for a holiday cheese board. To
that list of essential kitchen equipment (page 15), I should have included
the Microplane I use exclusively for grating parmesan—the shape of the
Microplane produces a fine dusting like a midwinter snowfall.

One of our favourite egg dishes for a cold morning is baked, or shirred,
eggs. The name comes from the "shirrer," the flat-bottomed ceramic dish
they're baked in. They're similar to the French oeufs en cocotte (eggs
cooked in ramekins in a bain marie) and something like a plain version
of a shakshuka, or a basic frittata (without the extra ingredients). You can
make them with just eggs and a bit of butter, but Sam and I like to add

a drop of whipping cream and top each dish with fresh bread crumbs and a dusting of parmesan. That makes it more of a gratin. And what isn't improved by a crust of parm?

To round out the meal, we serve them with bacon. But since we have the oven on already, we bake the bacon and do so using a trick from the kitchens of fancier brunch spots. It produces bacon that's as flat as a board—and less greasy than bacon prepared in a pan.

SERVES 4

· ·

Bacon (about 12 slices)

8 eggs

4 tablespoons butter

Pepper to taste

½ cup fresh bread crumbs

½ cup freshly grated parmesan

· ·

Preheat the oven to 400°F.

Line a baking sheet with foil. Place an oven-safe metal baking grid inside the lined baking sheet. Arrange a single layer of bacon on the rack, then place a second oven-safe metal grid on top of the bacon. Bake for 10 minutes or until most of the fat has rendered and the bacon has browned—longer for thicker bacon. Remove from the oven and, using tongs, place the cooked bacon on a couple of sheets of paper towel to cool. While the bacon is cooking, get the eggs ready for their turn in the oven.

Raise the oven temperature to 450°F. Butter the bottom and sides of four gratin dishes (each about 5 inches, enough to hold two eggs). Crack two eggs into each dish. Season with pepper, then sprinkle the bread crumbs and parmesan evenly over each dish of eggs. Place on a rack in the top third of the oven and bake until set, around 7 to 8 minutes.

TOAD IN A HOLE

There aren't many breakfast dish names that could potentially refer to two recipes that are light-years apart, but this is one of them. My mom's version of toad in a hole ("Come get your toad-in-a-hoooole!!") was what's more universal in North America: an egg fried sunny-side up in a circle cut from the centre of a piece of bread. It's so simple, it doesn't require more instruction than that, other than you should remember to use the leftover circle for scooping up the yolk.

The other version, which requires a bit more skill but is much more fun as a Sunday project, is a very English dish of sausages and Yorkshire pudding. Yorkshire pudding is itself an odd name, since a pudding in the U.K. usually refers to a kind of steamed or boiled dessert, whereas this pudding is baked from what's essentially a pancake batter and usually served alongside a main course. But why is the breakfast recipe called a toad in a hole? No one really knows. The first references to people eating a dish called toad in a hole appeared around the late 18th century. Baking a sausage or bits of beef in batter was one way to make a meal out of small amounts of meat. There's no evidence that anyone was baking actual toads. But at a glance, the sausages poking out of the baked pudding could resemble skittish toads peeking out of a hiding place.

This recipe is perhaps less kid-friendly to make than the North American version, inasmuch as you need to crank up the oven and spread the batter into a searing hot pan. That's Dad's job. The kid's job is to mix the batter, which they've already mastered for pancakes. You could easily make this for lunch or dinner, but the egginess of the pudding feels more breakfasty to me.

SERVES 4

· ·

6 small to medium farmer's sausages or any mild,
    herb-flavoured sausages
2 eggs
1 cup all-purpose flour
1⅓ cups whole milk
Pepper to taste
3 tablespoons vegetable oil or lard
1 tablespoon freshly grated parmesan
Worcestershire sauce (optional)

· ·

Preheat the oven to 425°F.

In a 12-inch cast-iron skillet on medium heat, fry the sausages until well browned, then set aside on a warm plate. (The skillet should be oven-safe—it will also be your baking dish.)

In a medium mixing bowl, mix together the eggs, flour, milk, and pepper (if you can complete this step the night before and leave the gluten to relax in the fridge until morning, that's ideal—and very proactive of you, congrats!).

Add the oil to the cast-iron skillet you used to fry the sausages. Place the skillet in the oven until the fat is moments away from smoking. Make sure you're wearing thick oven mitts for this next step: pull out the pan and quickly pour in the batter (it should sizzle). Then lower in the sausages, one by one, until they're evenly distributed. Sprinkle the cheese on top. Return to the oven. Bake for 30 minutes or until the batter has browned and puffed up like a hat. Avoid opening the door for a peek before the time is up, as it'll promptly deflate. Serve warm. If you like, anoint with a few drops of Worcestershire sauce.

SAUCY POACHED EGGS WITH FETA

A few years before Sam was born, a small group gathered for a weekend at a lakeside cottage. That winter, everyone seemed to be discovering a recipe by Yotam Ottolenghi and Sami Tamimi for shakshuka, the Tunisian dish of eggs poached with veg (potatoes and eggplant, usually) in tomatoes. At the cottage, we were promised a surprise treat for the weekend's final breakfast. That morning, after our host got the coffee going, he announced he was making shakshuka. For the first time. More than an hour later, the six of us were still hungrily waiting, surrounded by the scent of cooking tomatoes and spices. I'd made the mistake to volunteer for cleanup duty, only to realize that the over-ambitious cook had managed to use nearly every mixing bowl and cooking implement in the cottage, despite the fact that shakshuka has a good reputation as a one-pan wonder. I shouldn't complain, because when we finally got around to eating, it was one of the tastiest meals of the trip.

One more recent weekend, I cracked open *Jerusalem*, looking for shakshuka. But working against Sam's impatience, I made a few shortcuts, reduced the number of ingredients, and restrained the spices for a kid's palate. The main difference with my version is that I use passata instead of whole tomatoes, which cuts the cooking time down substantially. You could throw in a few diced cherry tomatoes to add some texture, if you like. In fact, the great thing about shakshuka is how adaptable the recipe is—some weekends I'll swap out the bell peppers for diced zucchini, roasted eggplant, or even corn niblets, which tips the recipe in the direction of huevos rancheros.

SERVES 4

• •

Olive oil, for frying

1 bell pepper (yellow or red), diced

1 shallot, diced

1 clove garlic, crushed

1 teaspoon ground coriander

1 teaspoon ground cumin

1 teaspoon salt

1 teaspoon freshly cracked pepper

1 jar (500 mL) passata

6 eggs

1 cup crumbled feta (goat or cow's milk)

4 to 8 whole wheat pita breads, toasted, for serving

Small tub plain yogurt, for serving

Sriracha, for serving (optional)

• •

In a large, deep-bottomed skillet or shallow, enamelled French oven, heat the oil to medium. Fry the peppers, shallots, garlic, coriander, cumin, salt, and pepper for 5 minutes or until the peppers begin to soften. Add the passata and mix everything together, then bring the pan down to a simmer for 10 minutes. If the sauce grows too thick, add small amounts of water.

Use a spatula to create six divots in the sauce. One by one, crack the eggs into the divots, making sure not to break the yolks. Simmer, uncovered, for another 10 minutes, until the whites are set but the yolks are still somewhat runny. Sprinkle the feta around the pan. Serve with toasted pita bread and yogurt. The sriracha is for any parent—or kid—who wants a bit more heat.

SUNDAY

17

EGGS BENEDICT AND HASH BROWNS

It took a while for people to recognize breakfast for what it is: the most important meal of the day. The ancient Greeks and Romans, with many temples to build and battles to wage, made a point of eating three square meals, though breakfast was usually leftovers from the night before. In the Middle Ages, they had second thoughts about eating before noon. The 13th-century theologian Thomas Aquinas, not known for his fun streak, identified breakfast as a gateway to sinful gluttony. Sneering at breakfast was as much a church as a class thing: the non-labourers like the clergy could keep fasting until later in the day because they didn't need the energy to till fields.

But that changed when chocolate, tea, and coffee arrived in continental Europe, and the Church, to avoid revolt, rewrote its rules to allow for the consumption of morning liquids (including a rich and creamy mug of hot chocolate). In other words, liquids didn't break the fast. From there it was a slippery, tea-slicked slope to Queen Elizabeth (the first one) consuming a loaf of bread, mutton stew, and jugs of ale, all before eight o'clock, and Samuel Pepys hosting his daybreak guests, as he noted in his prolific diaries, for "a barrel of oysters, a dish of neat's tongues, and a dish of anchovies, wine of all sorts, and Northdown ale." Not for the first time, what was once sinful became all the rage.

My idea of a gluttonous breakfast is less about quantity (though I'd happily join Pepys for that barrel of oysters) than the richness of the various parts. One of the most sinful options out there is a well-made eggs Benedict. The exact origins of the recipe are disputed, including where it got its name. I'd long assumed it had something to do with Benedict Arnold (surely a notorious traitor would be the kind of guy who'd pour hollandaise sauce on everything?), but I was very wrong. There's some agreement that the dish was first served in New York, though different restaurants claim to be behind it. One of the more persuasive stories has it that Charles Ranhofer, a chef at Delmonico's, a grand, old restaurant in Lower Manhattan, created eggs Benedict in the 1860s for a couple, Mr. and Mrs. LeGrand Benedict. They were frequent guests who one day, bored with the usual menu, asked for something new. Ranhofer included his recipe in *The Epicurean*, his 1894 cookbook.

There are a dozen ways to make eggs Benedict, but the basic elements are always a poached egg sitting on top of a slice of ham or pieces of bacon (or smoked salmon—which is called eggs royale, and gets a garnish of dill), which together rest on half a toasted English muffin, and the whole thing gets coated in hollandaise. I figure that if you're going to the trouble of making a hollandaise sauce, you should go all the way and replace the muffin with a fresh-baked, buttery biscuit. And, for that matter, serve your eggs Benedict with hot and just slightly greasy hash browns. This is a once-in-a-blue-moon dish—any more often and you'll risk gout and the wrath of Thomas Aquinas.

SERVES 4

· ·

For the biscuits

2 cups all-purpose flour

2½ teaspoons baking powder

1 teaspoon salt

4 tablespoons unsalted butter, cut into cubes

2 eggs

½ cup whipping cream (reserve 1 tablespoon)

1 tablespoon lemon zest

For the hollandaise

4 egg yolks

1 tablespoon lemon juice

½ cup melted unsalted butter

¼ teaspoon cayenne

For the hash browns

4 medium potatoes (Russet are ideal), washed and unpeeled

½ cup vegetable oil, divided

1 small onion, diced

Salt and pepper to taste

For the eggs Benedict

1 tablespoon oil

8 slices peameal bacon

1 tablespoon white vinegar

8 eggs

· ·

Preheat the oven to 425°F and line a baking sheet with parchment paper.

To make the biscuits, combine the flour, baking powder, and salt in a food processor with a dough blade. Add the butter and pulse until it resembles wet sand. Add the eggs, cream, and lemon zest and pulse until combined. (If you don't have a food processor or don't feel like cleaning all the parts after using one, you could also cut the butter into the dry ingredients in a large bowl, using two knives, and then mix the rest of the ingredients in with a wooden spoon. But the food processor finishes the job in a fraction of the time.)

Tip the mixture onto a floured countertop, then knead until it just comes together. Roll out the dough until 1 inch thick, then cut out circles (I use the floured rim of a 3-inch-wide tumbler) and place on the prepared baking sheet. Brush the top of each circle with the reserved cream. Bake for 20 minutes or until just starting to brown on top. Leave on a cooling rack while you prepare the rest of the dish.

To make the hollandaise, whisk the yolks and lemon juice in a stainless-steel bowl until they double in volume.

Meanwhile, simmer an inch of water in a medium saucepan. Place the bowl over the saucepan—pour out some water if it's high enough to touch the base of the bowl. Whisk the mixture, ensuring the eggs don't overheat and scramble, and gradually pour in the butter. When the mixture thickens to the consistency of pudding, remove from the heat and stir in the cayenne. Cover and set aside—you'll want it warm or at room temperature when you assemble the eggs Benedict.

To make the hash browns, shred the potatoes with a box grater. Immerse the shredded potatoes in a bowl of cool water, stir around to loosen the starches, then drain and repeat two more times. Squeeze out excess water, then dry the potatoes between two clean dish towels (this will help the potatoes crisp up better).

In a skillet over medium-high heat, heat ¼ cup oil. Cook the onions until translucent, then place them in a bowl. Heat the remaining ¼ cup oil in the skillet, then spread the potatoes evenly in the skillet and sprinkle salt and pepper overtop. Cook undisturbed for 4 to 5 minutes, until the bottom of the potatoes has started to form a crust. Using a spatula, break apart the potatoes into sections, flip, and cook for another 4 minutes. Add the onions back into the pan and mix with the potatoes.

To make the bacon, heat oil in a skillet over medium-high heat. Fry the bacon until browned and crisp, then set aside on paper towel to absorb the excess grease. (If you have more than one skillet, you could cook the bacon at the same time the potatoes are browning. If not, when the potatoes are finished, let that skillet cool slightly, then wipe or brush out any browned bits before reheating it for the bacon.)

Fill a wide, deep-bottomed saucepan halfway with water and bring to a boil. Add the vinegar (it helps keep the poaching eggs contained). On the edge of a bowl or your kitchen counter, crack one egg at a time and then gently drop the yolk and whites into the water—the goal is to keep the yolk unbroken and the whites close by, like the atmosphere around a young planet. Once all the eggs are in the saucepan, lower the heat to a simmer and cook for 3 minutes or until the whites are set. Remove carefully with a slotted spoon, placing the eggs on a warm plate.

To assemble the eggs Benedict, slice open the biscuits onto a plate. Layer one slice of bacon and one poached egg on each biscuit half. Ladle the warm hollandaise overtop. If the hollandaise has cooled and thickened, stir in a few drops of warm water before ladling (don't do this on the stove, as too much heat will split the sauce).

COTTAGE CHEESE AND SPINACH CASSEROLE

Family heirlooms have a way of accumulating and weighing you down in ways you don't expect. The effect on the brain is like a mortgage you'll never be able to pay off, until you pass that heirloom along to another unsuspecting family member. The credenza in our dining room contains two sets of brittle bone china. The petit-point floral-patterned set once belonged to my paternal grandmother, and the austerely white, gold-rimmed German set to my maternal grandmother. Each set includes more pieces than we need—we've never found an excuse to pull out the gherkin plate. We'll use one of the sets for holiday dinners, which is more than enough for plates that won't survive a run in the dishwasher. Otherwise they wait there in their dark cupboards, as useful as our collection of old modems in a box in the basement. (What for? I've no idea. Maybe we're waiting for someone to ask us to donate them to an obsolete tech museum.)

The one heirloom we find an excuse to use nearly every week is my mom's original Corning casserole dish with its pattern of blue cornflowers. It's not technically an heirloom—from the 1950s to the 1980s, nearly every couple in North America had that same casserole dish on their wedding registry. My mom gave me hers after she chipped the glass lid and decided to treat herself to a new one. I don't mind the chipped lid—it still works. That family casserole dish is treasured, mostly for how dependable it is, plus it gets used today, as much as it was used by Mom, to cook much more than casseroles. Unlike my grandmothers' china, you can stick it straight from the fridge into the oven or on a cooktop, and run it through the dishwasher. In my books that counts as an heirloom.

Sundays are prime casserole time. My favourite casserole recipe, which combines cottage cheese and spinach, is more of a brunch dish. If it doesn't disappear right away, it tastes even better as leftovers the next day (true of pretty much any casserole), after the baked cheese has had a chance to mellow.

SERVES 4 TO 6

· ·

1 package (11 ounces) washed baby spinach

8 tablespoons unsalted butter, divided

1 medium onion, chopped

3 cloves garlic, minced

2 cups full-fat cottage cheese

6 eggs

3 cups grated white cheddar or Monterey Jack

Salt and pepper to taste

¼ cup panko bread crumbs

Bread for toast, for serving (optional)

· ·

In a covered medium pot, steam the spinach until wilted (the water clinging to the leaves from its washing should suffice to build up steam), then drain thoroughly. Meanwhile, melt 2 tablespoons butter in a skillet and fry the onions and garlic until the onions are just translucent. Set aside to cool.

Preheat your oven to 350°F.

In a small bowl, melt the remaining butter in the microwave. In a mixing bowl, combine the melted butter, cottage cheese, eggs, cheese, salt, and pepper. Stir in the cooled vegetables and mix until well combined. At this stage, you could also mix in a tablespoon of flour to help the casserole cohere if you think you didn't quite drain enough of the water from the spinach.

Pour the mixture into a well-buttered 3-quart casserole dish. Sprinkle the bread crumbs evenly across the surface. Bake for 45 minutes, uncovered, or until the top is lightly browned. I usually let the casserole rest for 5 minutes after taking it from the oven, and serve it with toast.

Leftovers will keep for a couple of days, covered, in the fridge.

DIY CREAM OF WHEAT

As chilly morning warm-ups go, this one takes top prize. The dense porridge seems to hold onto the heat from the stove forever. It always fills our bellies with a cozy happiness. Cream of wheat is also a convenient vessel for whatever kind of topping you want to stir into it. Most days all we need is a pat of butter and maybe a small spoonful of brown sugar. Anything more, and you start to lose track of its essential creaminess and wheatiness. The other great pleasure of cream of wheat is spooning through the elasticky skin that forms on the surface as it cools.

Even better than cream of wheat from a box is cream of wheat that you've made yourself. The process sounds needlessly complicated when the store-bought version is perfectly fine, but believe me, it's worth the extra effort. To start, you need to find whole wheat berries. Most health food or bulk stores will have them. You can also try farro, which is another kind of whole wheat more typically grown around the Mediterranean. Fresh-ground wheat berries, unlike the boxed cream of wheat, still contain wheat germ, which gives the cooked porridge a deeper, nuttier flavour. The first time I tried making my own, I was like a certain tornado-tossed Kansas teen waking up to the world in colour.

If you've never ground your own wheat before, be prepared for a bit of a mess. You'll need a grain mill (I use an attachment to my stand mixer), but if you don't plan on grinding grains all the time, you can easily use a blender or coffee grinder instead. If you do like the idea of grinding wheat, you'll find yourself looking for excuses to use the grain mill, the best of which is to freshly grind your own wheat for homemade bread.

SERVES 2 TO 3

· ·

1 cup wheat berries or farro

4 cups milk

1 teaspoon salt

Toppings of your choice: A pat of butter is a good start.
Then branch out to brown sugar, maple syrup, fresh berries,
a spoonful of jam, or banana slices.

· ·

Grind the wheat berries until they resemble dry, grainy sand. This could take 5 to 10 minutes, depending on the strength of your mixer or blender.

In a medium pot, bring the milk to a simmer—be sure to avoid letting it come to a full boil. Gradually pour in the wheat and salt, and immediately whisk vigorously to avoid clumping. Lower the heat and cook for about 5 minutes or until the mixture begins to thicken. Immediately remove from the heat, whisking as you do. Pour into cereal bowls and add your preferred toppings.

CINNAMON SQUARE CEREAL

Many mornings, Sam hops out of bed and taps on his iPad to find his cartoons. He'll act like we're torturing him when we turn it off and push him toward the kitchen table. And he'll ask why he can't have his bowl of cereal on the floor, watching his show. The one time I tried to convince him that breakfast is the most important meal of the day, he threw down that all-purpose kid's gauntlet and asked "Why?"

It turns out the saying first gained real traction in the late 19th century because of one of the early inventors of cereal: John Harvey Kellogg. A rigid Seventh-day Adventist, he claimed his Corn Flakes, by virtue of being so dry and plain, kept your mind clean of temptations such as masturbation (one of his special preoccupations). Despite that compelling sales pitch, boxed cereals only really took off when many women filled men's vacated jobs during World War I. They needed something quick and easy to serve their families each morning. After WWII, bacon marketers took up the "most important meal of the day" idea and encouraged doctors to tout high-protein breakfasts as better for you than a box of wheat. And so bacon and two (or, even better, three) eggs became the new ideal of the North American breakfast, along with middle-class suburban houses with breakfast rooms, a glass of OJ made from a frozen concentrate, and two and a half kids warned never to bother Dad while he's reading his morning paper.

I can only imagine what John Harvey Kellogg would think of what became of his Corn Flakes company. Corn Flakes begat Frosted Flakes, which begat Frosted Mini-Wheats, Corn Pops, Apple Jacks, Honey Smacks, and Froot Loops. It's no small challenge to steer a kid away from the cereal aisle at the grocery store, where Sam has had his share of meltdowns. I've had some luck convincing him that we don't need to buy whatever new box has caught his eye when together we can make our own. Making your own cereal sounds like a fool's errand when the store-bought options are generally so cheap and easy. (I can imagine those WWI women workers rolling their eyes at the idea. And modern-day frazzled parents too.) But hear me out: by making your own cereal you can control how much sugar it contains, not to mention that you'll be avoiding whatever preservatives and shelf-stabilizer additives coat the manufactured options.

There's no shortage of online recipes for homemade versions of everything from Froot Loops to Cheerios, and many of them are designed with gluten intolerance in mind. Through my close studies with Sam, we decided our favourite homemade cereal is a riff on widely shared online recipes for Cinnamon Toast Crunch. Sam is a fan of anything involving cinnamon. When we warm apple cider in the fall, he'll pull out the cinnamon stick and suck on it for hours. Crunchy cinnamon cereal sweetened with a bit of sugar was an easy sell.

Our recipe yields about five cups. That's enough for two or three breakfasts, depending on how many bowls you eat in one sitting, though it also makes a good snack and it rarely lasts more than a couple of days. It's faster to make with a food processor, but if you don't have one it's still easily mixed by hand.

SERVES 4

• •

1 cup lightly packed light brown sugar

2 tablespoons cinnamon, divided

2½ cups whole wheat pastry flour

2½ cups all-purpose flour

1 teaspoon salt

2 cups unsalted butter, diced in small cubes

1 tablespoon granulated sugar

1 tablespoon vanilla paste

1 cup ice water

¼ cup melted butter

• •

In a bowl, combine the brown sugar and 1 tablespoon cinnamon. In
a food processor fitted with a pastry blade, blend the whole wheat flour,
all-purpose flour, remaining 1 tablespoon cinnamon, and salt. Add the
butter, granulated sugar, and vanilla, then pulse until the mixture
resembles clumpy wet sand. Slowly add the ice water until a dough forms.
Tip onto a lightly floured counter and gently bring together. Divide into
four balls, then wrap in plastic wrap and refrigerate for 30 minutes—no
more than an hour.

Preheat the oven to 350°F.

Lightly cover four baking-sheet-size pieces of parchment paper with flour.
Cover a rolling pin in flour (you'll need to redo this a few times while
you're preparing the dough). Starting with one ball of dough, roll out
evenly, moving from the centre outward, until it forms something
approximating a rectangle, and not thicker than ¼ inch. Carefully pull
the paper and dough onto a baking sheet. Repeat this with the three
remaining balls of dough.

Brush the surface of the rolled-out dough with melted butter and sprinkle each piece of dough with a quarter of the brown sugar–cinnamon mixture. Careful to avoid slicing the parchment paper, use a steak knife or pizza cutter to cut the dough into 1-inch squares. You'll get about 24 squares per sheet of dough. Create a bit of space between each square. Bake on the middle rack, turning once so they are evenly brown, for 15 minutes.

Lifting the parchment, transfer the baked squares to a cooling rack. Once cooled, store in an airtight container (or an extra-large zippered plastic bag) for up to a week.

CHOCOLATE RICE PUDDING

Kids stuck in bed or in front of the TV with a cold are no small challenge to feed. Their taste buds and queasy stomachs can handle only so much. On the menu: plain toast and flat ginger ale. Maybe a bowl of low-sodium chicken soup, hold the pepper. For good measure, Mom would heat up a pot of rice pudding. Rice pudding is not generally recognized for its healing properties, but it can be comfortingly bland, and it's full of fibre and nutrients, not to mention milk proteins, so why not? Rice pudding is also sweet in a way that kids can never turn down, which is probably why I followed my mom's example and started making it for Sam whenever he got a cold too. He quickly figured out that if he wanted to get a bowl, he only had to act sniffly.

Rice pudding is also a breakfast staple, especially in the Philippines. Filipino champorado is made with sticky (glutinous) rice and chocolate (usually the dark unsweetened chocolate discs sold in Latin food stores) and finished with a swirl of condensed milk. It's often served with salted fish, which may sound strange to non-Filipinos but makes for a lot of sense as a savoury balance to the intense sweetness of the chocolate and milk. My version of rice pudding, like champorado, uses short-grain rice and mixes in chocolate. Instead of a side of fish, we sprinkle the top with flakes of salt.

SERVES 2 TO 4

• •

1 cup short-grain rice (arborio is ideal)

2 cups canned light coconut milk

½ teaspoon fine salt

¼ cup lightly packed brown sugar

¼ cup cocoa powder

1 cup coconut cream

Maldon salt to finish

• •

In a medium pot, heat the rice, coconut milk, and salt. When it reaches a simmer, cover with a lid and reduce the temperature to low, cooking for 30 minutes or until the liquid is mostly absorbed. When the rice and milk are creamy and thick, add the sugar, cocoa powder, and coconut cream, stirring to combine. Spoon into bowls and sprinkle with salt. Serve immediately.

BIRTHDAY BREAKFAST

In our kitchen, we have one shelf of cookbooks we use every week. And then we have shelves (and yet many more shelves) in a hallway filled with cookbooks that I bought to read but have no real plans to cook from. They're escapist books—ideas for cooking projects I might take up one day, way in the future, or overly complicated recipes I read once for amusement, then put back on the shelf.

One such escapist book is *Country Weekends*, the 1983 recipe collection by the American writer Lee Bailey. *Country Weekends* reads like a handbook for the 1 percent, with tips on what to serve (or order your staff to serve) under an arbour, on the boat dock, or while taking a break from show jumping. It's not totally useless: it does list some excellent recipes for strawberry shortcakes and, a special treat, grapefruit sherbet with candied grapefruit rind. Plus, it includes an outrageous idea for a "hearty breakfast" that has, with some adjustments, become my go-to for when it's my or Stephen's birthday. Sam would prefer we were making breakfast for his own birthday, but he also likes helping make it for one of his dads.

In Bailey's original menu, which he says was inspired by a typical meal from his childhood, he prepares quail—quail!—with grits, eggs, biscuits, and two types of homemade preserves. Even for a birthday, finding small game bird is a stretch. In my version I settle for scrambled eggs and buttermilk biscuits, adding cheddar and rosemary to the latter. And instead of quail, I roast a chicken for dinner the night before and warm the leftovers, which always taste better the next day.

For an extra-festive birthday, we'll toast with mimosas or Bellinis— and help Sam feel included by pouring a few glugs of fizzy water into his apple juice.

SERVES 4

• •

For the buttermilk biscuits

1 cup all-purpose flour

1 teaspoon baking powder

½ teaspoon baking soda

1 teaspoon salt

3 tablespoons unsalted butter, cubed

1 cup buttermilk

¼ cup grated white cheddar

1 tablespoon chopped fresh rosemary

For the scrambled eggs

1 tablespoon butter

8 eggs

1 teaspoon salt

1 teaspoon pepper

¼ cup whipping cream

½ cup grated white cheddar

½ leftover roast chicken (optional)

• •

Preheat the oven to 450°F. Line a baking sheet with parchment paper.

In a food processor fitted with a pastry blade, combine the flour, baking powder, baking soda, and salt. Add the butter and briefly process until you get a coarse mixture. Drizzle in the buttermilk and blend for 1 minute or until the dough starts to come together.

Tip the mixture onto a lightly floured countertop. Sprinkle the cheese and rosemary across the surface of the dough, then briefly knead together until combined. Using your hands, pull off puck-size chunks of the dough and place them on the prepared baking sheet. You should get 10 to 12 biscuits. Bake for 12 minutes or until the tops are lightly browned.

While the biscuits are cooling, start making the eggs. Heat the butter in a large skillet on medium, spreading it with a spatula so it evenly coats the surface.

In a mixing bowl, whisk together the eggs, salt, pepper, and cream until frothy. Add the eggs to the skillet and, using a spatula, slowly stir the eggs in a figure eight so the uncooked and cooked parts combine, until the eggs start to become more solid. While the eggs are still creamy, sprinkle in the cheese and stir. Just before the eggs become firm, remove from the heat.

Serve the eggs with the warm biscuits. If you planned ahead and roasted a chicken the night before, warm sliced leftovers and serve on the side.

THE GREATEST GRANOLA

Before granola became a thing that we give as gifts in ribboned Mason jars, it was a miracle cure. In the 1860s, James Caleb Jackson, a doctor at a health spa in upstate New York, needed a healthy breakfast for his patients. At the time, a proper morning meal consisted of eggs, meat, and toast, and more eggs, meat, and toast. Jackson's radical idea was to cure his patients of their gout, and other well-to-do ailments, by changing what they ate. For breakfast he gave them graham flour baked into brittle cakes, broken up and served soaked in cold milk. He essentially created the first manufactured cereal. Some of his patients referred to it as "wheat rocks," but Jackson preferred the name "granula," after the granules formed by the broken graham. When John Harvey Kellogg, who was running his own health spa, copied the recipe, Jackson sued. Kellogg in turn changed the name of his cereal (made with oats, wheat flour, and corn flour, for good measure) to granola. Cereal historians, if there were such a profession, would also point out that a doctor was serving his Zurich sanatorium patients a granola-like breakfast cereal called muesli around the same time.

Most granola sold today wouldn't qualify as healthy in a spa in Zurich, upstate New York, or anywhere else. The main reason: it's often liberally coated in brown sugar, which makes all that baked wheat and graham flour go down easier. But it's possible, and in fact very easy, to make your own granola, and to make one that tastes delicious without any processed sugars. In our house Stephen has become the granola king. He originally started making it during one of his healthy eating kicks, then kept making it, and we kept eating it, because it was too good not to do so. It's sweetened with apple juice and dates instead of with processed sugars. The handful of chocolate nibs don't hurt either. The list of ingredients is long but easy to find at most bulk or natural food stores. To get the granola just the right consistency, it's important to bake it low and slow. The house fills with the wonderful scent of toasting nuts, dried fruit, and chocolate. Stephen always makes a giant batch, but it rarely lasts long.

MAKES 12 CUPS GRANOLA (SERVES 10 TO 12)

• •

3 cups unsweetened apple juice

20 dates, pitted and diced

2 tablespoons cinnamon

1 tablespoon vanilla paste

3 cups pecans

2 cups almonds

1 cup cashews

1½ cups pepitas

½ cup dried goji berries

½ cup dried cranberries

½ cup diced dried apricots

½ cup white sesame seeds

½ cup black sesame seeds

½ cup cacao nibs

1½ cups desiccated unsweetened coconut

1½ cups almond meal

1 tablespoon sea salt, or to taste

• •

Preheat the oven to 180°F. Line two baking sheets with parchment paper.

In a medium saucepan, stir together the apple juice, dates, cinnamon, and vanilla. Simmer for 15 minutes. Pour into a stand mixer and blend until smooth.

In a mixing bowl, combine the pecans, almonds, cashews, pepitas, goji berries, cranberries, apricots, white sesame seeds, black sesame seeds, cacao nibs, coconut, and almond meal. Pour the juice mixture over the dry ingredients and mix until everything is damp and clumping together.

Divide and spread the granola among the prepared baking sheets, tamp down with the back of a spoon until evenly distributed, and then bake for 2½ hours. Midway through, take the sheets out and break up the granola, flipping chunks over to expose the wetter parts. If the granola isn't dried out and toasted after the full time, return it to the oven for another 20 to 30 minutes.

Sprinkle with the salt. Let cool, then seal in airtight plastic bags or containers. It'll keep for a full month.

BLUEBERRY PIEROGI

For one lost summer in my 20s, I worked at an Eastern European café next door to my university. As students, we went there to sip cheap coffee or, after classes, pitchers of cheap beer. The staff—so miserable, they seemed cool—yelled at each other over the shriek of the espresso machine.

I considered myself undeservingly lucky when a roommate's elder sister, who was one of the sneering staff, got me a part-time job at the café's prepared foods counter. Summer jobs can clarify what you want to get out of life. I was responsible for ladling bowls of borscht and plates of mashed potatoes to customers who stood in a silent line and pointed at what they wanted, as if they were back in socialist Eastern Europe. As the summer days grew long and hot, I was also tasked with preparing lemon iced tea, one of the priciest items on the menu, which I discovered was just water and powdered Nestea from an industrial-size can. My manager, wary of revealing company secrets, pushed me into a backroom to do my Nestea mixing. It was there, flustered and sweating as I cranked the handheld can opener, that the lid suddenly popped upright and I sliced the palm of my right hand. Calling me an idiot, which felt mean at the time but was probably accurate, he ordered me downstairs to the office, where they kept bandages.

I had no idea where the office was located, so I started opening random doors. The farther I wandered the steamier it became. I was about to give up when I turned a corner and found myself standing in the middle of a circle of grandmas in kitchen smocks and kerchiefs. They were humming in unison and moving their limbs at a dizzying pace. One was stirring a massive pot of boiling water, which I realized was the source of the heat. Two were sitting with white buckets between their knees, into which they dropped potato peels. Others were kneading and rolling out dough. I'd stumbled into the café's pierogi factory. One of the women glanced at me and my elevated hand wrapped in a blood-soaked kitchen rag, and pointed to a door at my back—the office with the bandages.

A few days later the same kind woman found me at the hot counter. She handed me a small plate, turned, and left without a word. On the plate were three pierogi, still hot from the pot. I blew on one and took a bite. Inside, instead of the usual potato and cheese, it was sweet and filled with tiny blueberries. It was delicious.

After that summer I avoided restaurant jobs. I wasn't cut out for it. But I couldn't shake my taste for pierogi. I later moved into the city's Polish neighbourhood, in part so I could be closer to its bakeries and hot takeout counters. After a few practice runs, pierogi are a fun and easy cooking project—when you have a few hours. (In fact, if you're going to the effort, you might want to double or triple this recipe and freeze the leftovers, which keep for a couple of months.)

I found pierogi tips and inspiration from a few home cooks, but mainly from the Marja Ochorowicz-Monatowa's *Polish Cookery*, which is Poland's equivalent of the *Joy of Cooking*. For dinner, I've made them stuffed with wild mushrooms and duck confit, with shallots and blue cheese, and with the traditional cottage cheese. My specialty, though, is blueberry breakfast pierogi, which are also Sam's favourite. They're best when you're in the mood for an extra-hearty morning treat.

MAKES 24 PIEROGI (SERVES 4)

• •

2 cups all-purpose flour, divided

1 tablespoon powdered sugar, plus more for dusting

1 egg

1 cup warm water

1½ cups frozen blueberries (frozen are better than fresh for this recipe)

2 tablespoons granulated sugar

¼ teaspoon cinnamon

1 teaspoon lemon zest

Butter, for frying (optional)

Plain yogurt, for dipping

• •

Sift together the flour and powdered sugar. Place in the bowl of a stand mixer fitted with a dough arm and, on low speed, gradually add the egg and water until the dough just comes together. Tip onto a floured counter and form into a ball, then knead for about 5 minutes until it becomes more elastic (doing this part by hand helps you avoid over-kneading it). Return the dough to the mixer bowl, cover with a damp cloth, and let rest for an hour.

In a medium bowl, mix the blueberries with the sugar, cinnamon, and lemon zest, and set aside.

On a floured surface, cut the dough in two and, working with one section at a time, roll out until slightly thicker than a quarter. Rub the rim of a 3-inch-wide juice glass with flour and cut out circles from the rolled dough. As you're working, place the circles on a sheet of parchment paper and cover with a damp tea towel.

—→

Now, to fill and assemble the pierogi it's easiest to place a circle in the palm of your hand (assuming you've no Nestea can injuries to speak of) and, using a spoon, place a half-dozen blueberries in the centre (more if the blueberries are the small wild variety). Fold the circle over, pinching to form a seal. Place the completed pierogi back on the parchment paper and under the towel until you're ready for the next step.

At this stage, the formed pierogi can be frozen for up to a month (I recommend freezing them on a baking sheet and then sealing the frozen pastries in a large freezer bag). Or you could cook them. To do so, bring a pot of water to a vigorous boil. Gently lower the fresh or frozen pierogi into the water. When they float to the surface, they're ready.

If you like your pierogi crisp, you can go a further step and fry the drained pierogi in a buttery skillet until both sides are lightly browned. I like them either way. For breakfast, I always dust them with a spoon of powdered sugar and drop a dollop of plain yogurt on each plate, for dipping.

DIY YOGURT AND 1980s FRUIT SALAD

There's a long list of things we regularly eat that we don't need to make ourselves but, when we do so, deliver more than an ounce of smug satisfaction. For instance, I'm lucky to have good bakeries nearby, yet I still end up baking my own sourdough. Once you start, you're not really allowed to stop baking sourdough unless you're okay to let your sourdough starter die of neglect. The same thing is true of making yogurt. No one truly needs to make yogurt, not when the supermarket dairy aisle has dozens of options—sweet and tart, thick and thin, Greek and Icelandic style. But when you make yogurt yourself, it does taste fresher, creamier, and more flavourful than anything you can buy. Making it yourself also lets you control what goes into it—in particular, the quality of the milk, but also the fruit and other add-ins. The best part is, you can get into a routine of making exactly how much you need for you and your family for the week, so you'll never go without. And you can add it to the list of home science experiments to run with your kid.

Making your own yogurt can get very complicated very fast, with all kinds of gadgets, special yogurt makers, and the fanatical sterilization of equipment. In my recipe, I've aimed to keep the complications to a minimum while still ending up with a consistently delicious yogurt. I never guessed I could so easily make my own yogurt out of a couple of litres of milk—it's the dairy equivalent of a card trick.

If I'm not mixing my yogurt with granola (see page 103), I'll usually round out the breakfast with fresh fruit. I recently resuscitated what I call 1980s Fruit Salad, which is defined by canned fruits and sweetened with simple syrup.

MAKES 8 CUPS YOGURT AND 6 CUPS FRUIT SALAD (SERVES 6 TO 8)

• •

For the yogurt (makes 8 cups)

8 cups whole milk (see note)

1 cup non-fat milk powder

½ cup store-bought yogurt (see note)

1 cup seasonal fruit, to mix in (see note, optional)

½ cup other fixings, to mix in (maple syrup, honey, or homemade jams) (optional)

For the fruit salad

½ cup granulated sugar

½ cup water

3 kiwis, peeled and sliced into eighths

4 mandarin oranges, peeled and segmented (canned is okay, and in fact more authentic)

2 cups seedless grapes, halved

2 apples, diced into cubes (aim for sweeter, like Gala or Honeycrisp)

1 cup pineapple chunks (fresh or, again, canned is okay)

• •

Start by running four 16-ounce Mason jars and their lids, a whisk, and a spatula through your dishwasher, set to the sterilize cycle. For good measure, wash your 5-quart Dutch oven with scalding hot water and a lot of soap, then rinse well.

Preheat the oven to 90°F. Attach an oven-safe thermometer to the Dutch oven. On your stovetop, heat the milk and milk powder to 180°F (don't let it boil), whisking frequently to avoid burning. Heating the milk prepares its proteins for yogurt-ization. Let the milk cool to 115°F (to speed this up, you can partially immerse the Dutch oven in an ice bath in your sink). Now comes the crucial step: in a mixing bowl, whisk a cup of the warm milk with the store-bought yogurt until combined. Quickly pour the milk-yogurt mixture into the pot, whisking until it's evenly distributed, then cover the pot with its lid, wrap it in tea towels, and place it in the preheated oven. Turn the oven off and leave the yogurt to work its magic for a minimum of 4 hours. You can occasionally open the lid and check its progress, but I avoid doing so: your goal is to keep what's inside the pot at a near-constant 110°F.

The yogurt is set when it looks solidly creamy (there's an oxymoron!). Ladle it into Mason jars and set aside to cool. The yogurt will keep for 2 weeks in the fridge. Remember to save at least ½ cup of your yogurt to start your next batch. And on it goes!

At breakfast, add the optional fresh fruit and other fixings, to taste, to individual bowls of yogurt.

Fruit salad should be made at least half an hour before you're planning to eat it. The preparation is simple enough to handle before you've even had your morning coffee. In a small pot, bring the sugar and water to a simmer, stirring until fully dissolved. Set aside to cool.

Gently mix the fruit in a serving bowl. Pour in ¼ cup of cooled syrup to start (decide how much you want to use—the syrup will keep in the fridge for 3 weeks). Stir until the fruit is evenly coated.

Notes:

(1) Organic milk from a small dairy is best, if you can find it, since it'll contain more milk proteins than the equivalent from an industrial producer.

(2) The store-bought yogurt is the starter that'll kick off your homemade version, and after this you'll use your own yogurt to make the next batch.

(3) When it comes to seasonal fruit, I like Cara Cara oranges or clementines in winter, berries and stone fruit come summer, and poached apples and pears in fall.

CAPE BRETON COD CAKES
AND CHOW-CHOW

My in-laws live above the cliffs on the Cape Breton coast, where the Atlantic winds whip through the stubby trees and, in the distance, the Newfoundland ferry chugs on the horizon. We usually time our visits to Sam's birthday, which coincides with the tail end, so to speak, of lobster season. His grandfather (we call him "papa") pulls the propane boiler out of the shed and boils the crustaceans beside their back deck. Nan (Sam's grandma) spreads a plastic tablecloth across the dining table, and everyone crowds around for lobster with butter, buns, and usually a bowl of potato salad too.

I love my in-laws, but we'd still make those trips just for the seafood. We always save a day to drive the Cabot Trail, which winds along the oceanside cliffs and deposits you in the Acadian fishing village of Cheticamp, for sparkling oysters and steamed crab.

My absolute favourite East Coast dish is one of the humblest: the cod cake. At my in-laws' house, cod cakes are more popular than hamburgers. The traditional method is to use salted cod (i.e., cod that's been dehydrated and preserved in salt). If you do, the fillets need to be soaked overnight in a saucepan and well drained. Fans of salted cod will tell you that it's more flavourful and sweeter than its fresh counterpart. Back at home, on my lazier weekends, I'll opt for fresh fillets of any flaky white fish that's available at my nearby fishmonger or supermarket. Buttery, flakier fish also goes over easier with kids.

There are no hard rules for what to serve with cod cakes, but for breakfast they go well with biscuits and fried eggs, or with a small green salad. More often than not, I'll pull out a jar of chow-chow, a sharp, vinegary relish of green tomatoes and onions, and sometimes peppers, that's as popular in the Acadian towns of Nova Scotia as it is among the Cajuns of Louisiana. Making chow-chow is a full afternoon activity—it'll eat up a solid two to three hours, between boiling the veg in vinegar and sterilizing jars. But kids always seem impressed that we can make at home something they usually see only on the shelves at a store. The chow-chow is ready to eat once made, but tastes better if you let it sit for a week or more. Plus, it's only worth the effort to make chow-chow if you're going to make enough to last the year. Jars of chow-chow also make a handy gift for friends—especially if those friends share your seafood obsession.

SERVES 6

For the chow-chow

4 cups diced green tomatoes

1 red tomato, diced

6 medium onions, diced

1 red bell pepper, diced

3 tablespoons salt

8 cups cider vinegar

5 cups granulated sugar

½ cup pickling spice

For the cod cakes

1 pound cod or haddock fillets

1 bay leaf

2 shallots or 1 small onion, diced

1 teaspoon plus ½ cup vegetable
oil, divided

5 medium Yukon Gold potatoes,
peeled and diced

1 egg

Salt and pepper to taste

A few pats of butter

To make the chow-chow, place the diced tomatoes, onions, peppers, and salt in a deep bowl. Cover with water, soak overnight, drain, and rinse.

In a large pot (I use a pasta pot), bring the vinegar and sugar to a boil. Add the vegetables and pickling spice tied up in a pickling bag. (If you don't have a pickling bag, you can double up a 12-inch square of cheesecloth, form a pouch, and tie it closed with twine. It's easier than it sounds.) Boil the vegetables until they're soft but not dissolving.

Divide the pickled vegetables into eight 2-cup sterilized pickling jars, leaving ½ inch of space at the top. Screw on the lids and leave to cool— when the lids "pop" that means they're sealed. The chow-chow is ready to eat, but will grow tarter and more delicious after a week. Store in a cool, dark cupboard for up to a year.

To make the cod cakes, place the fillets in a large skillet with the bay leaf. Fill with water until the fish is just covered. Heat to a simmer and cook until the fish is poached through (about 4 to 5 minutes). Remove with a slotted spatula and set aside in a deep mixing bowl—it doesn't matter if the fish breaks apart (and it will).

While the fish is boiling, gently fry the shallots in a teaspoon of oil in a small pan until just translucent, then let cool in the same mixing bowl.

Fill the large skillet again with water to cover the potatoes. Boil until starting to fall apart, about 10 minutes. Drain, let cool, and add to the mixing bowl with the fish.

Now comes the fun part. Add the egg, salt, and pepper to the potato fish mixture, then mix by hand, making sure the fish and vegetables are evenly distributed. Form into patties (you should get 8 to 10). Place the patties on a plate, uncovered, in the fridge for a minimum of half an hour, which helps them cohere and keep their shape for the next step.

Preheat the oven to 250°F.

In a skillet over medium heat, heat the ½ cup oil and the butter. When the butter has fully melted, gently position the patties evenly around the pan. You'll likely need to do this in two batches—four or five patties at a time. Fry until they form a crust, then flip and do the same with the other side. Keep the first batch on a baking sheet in a warm oven.

Serve the cakes garnished with the chow-chow. Leftover cakes will keep for a day in the fridge; lightly wrap in a paper towel to reheat in the microwave.

MINI PANCAKES

I discovered the golden rule about pancakes in a castle. In the early 1980s, my grandmother remarried. Her name is Oie, which means "flower," but ever since she'd landed in Canada as a young girl, having fled the 1940 Soviet annexation of Estonia, she'd been known as Eva, which was easier for Canadians to pronounce. She's our fun grandma, the one who is always the first to jump in the pool or bake us treats. Her new husband, Tonu, another World War II refugee, was a contractor who had built himself a sprawling stone house with a stout turret, modelled on the medieval castles back in the old country. His little castle was an hour north of Toronto, an eyesore between dairy farms that nevertheless was totally awesome to us kids. One weekend, our parents took us for a sleepover. While the adults had drinks, my brother and I stomped through muddy fields, leaping over cow patties and hunting for the Ark of the Covenant (the first Indiana Jones movie was still in theatres). That night we slept in the room at the top of the turret and decided we were made for castle life.

The next morning, Grandma Oie was first up, whisking batter in the kitchen. She instructed me to grab a stool at the island. I watched as she poured a small "test" pancake onto the frying pan, left it to bubble and crisp up, flipped it, then gave it to me for my formal evaluation. It was thicker than a crêpe but still thinner and eggier than the conventional pancakes we had at home. There was also a hint of spice—cinnamon? That delicious pancake disappeared in two quick bites. The full-size pancakes she made next were good but nowhere near as great as that tiny tester. I asked for the very last pancake in the batch, which was also small, made from the final scrape of batter from the mixing bowl. It was also awesome. Here was a rule: when it comes to pancakes, smaller is often better. Smaller means an ideal ratio of crispy, golden edge to pillowy centre. The smaller ones soak up the perfect amount of butter from the pan too. And they cook faster and more evenly than bigger pancakes, which seem to dry out if you leave them on the pan a second too long.

This wasn't an original discovery. People have long been calling these teeny-tiny pancakes "silver dollars," after the rare coin. They're a close relation to blinis. The way to achieve a perfect small pancake is to use a wet, heavier batter, with a fraction of the usual leavening agents—you don't want them to puff up too much. I also like to replenish the butter in the pan with nearly every batch of pancakes to ensure maximum buttery crispiness. If Sam and Stephen are in an extra-hungry mood, I'll double the recipe. Another discovery: smaller pancakes disappear faster.

SERVES 4

● ●

1¾ cups all-purpose flour

2 teaspoons baking powder

2 eggs

2 cups whole milk

2 tablespoons melted butter

2 tablespoons granulated sugar

½ teaspoon vanilla paste

¼ teaspoon nutmeg

½ teaspoon cinnamon

½ teaspoon salt

Butter, for frying

½ pound peameal bacon
  (optional)

Maple syrup, for serving

● ●

In a medium bowl, sift together the flour and baking powder. In a separate large bowl (with a spout, if that's an option), whisk the eggs, milk, melted butter, sugar, vanilla, nutmeg, cinnamon, and salt until very smooth. Pour in the dry ingredients and mix until just combined. Cover and leave in the fridge for 30 minutes or, even better, overnight.

Melt a tablespoon of butter in a large skillet over medium-high heat. Pour in a heaping tablespoon of batter per pancake, flipping over when the edges start to look crisp and the centre begins to dry, for a total of 2 to 3 minutes. Repeat until you have about two dozen pancakes.

When I'm halfway through the batter, I heat a second skillet to medium-high, melt some butter, and then fry the peameal bacon.

Deliver hot to the table with a bottle of maple syrup.

CHERRY CROSTATA

I have a habit of hunting through used bookstores for out-of-print cookbooks, or spiral-bound passion projects by a local home cook in a very specific subgenre of cookery (many of the best pickling guides fall into that category). The first thing I do is flip through, looking for the last owner's scribbled notations about recipes, which often help you make something even better. Home cooks helping home cooks. Sometimes the previous owner will have forgotten between the pages more recipes clipped from other sources or even a handwritten recipe card.

One such found gem that's become a personal favourite is by Paul Bertolli, the former chef at Chez Panisse, the California restaurant that influenced a thousand other restaurants. Someone had clipped his recipe for a cherry crostata from *Food & Wine* and carefully taped it into the back sleeve of a second-hand copy I found of *Chez Panisse Cooking*, among the best cooking guides to come out of the 1980s. Crostatas are fruit pies with a shortcrust—the Italian version of a galette. The crust is usually rustic and hand-formed, though I've encountered crostatas with neat edges and a precisely symmetrical lattice topping. Bertolli doesn't specify the type of cherries, only that they be "fresh," and after rounds of testing I decided this crostata works best with sour cherries, whose tartness marries well with the buttery pastry and the sweetened almonds. I'll bake it in summer, when sour cherries are in season, as the finale of a Sunday brunch menu, perhaps after Parmesan Shirred Eggs and Flat Bacon (page 73). Midsummer, replace the cherries with slices of tart nectarine.

SERVES 6

• •

2 cups plus 1 tablespoon all-purpose flour, divided

3 tablespoons granulated sugar, divided

½ teaspoon salt

¾ cup unsalted butter, diced and kept chilled in the fridge

½ cup cold water

2 tablespoons slivered blanched almonds

4 cups sour cherries, pitted

1 tablespoon butter, melted

• •

To make the pastry, mix the 2 cups flour, 1 tablespoon sugar, and salt in a food processor with a pastry blade. Gradually add the butter, pulsing as you go. Then gradually drizzle in the water (you might not need all of it) and pulse until the dough collects together. Dump the contents onto a floured counter, gather, and lightly knead until it starts to become elastic. Shape into a disc, cover in plastic wrap, and leave to rest in the fridge for an hour. While the dough is resting, preheat your oven to 400°F.

Chop the almonds into small pieces and combine in a small bowl with 1 tablespoon each of flour and sugar.

Now it's time to roll the dough. Rub a rolling pin with flour and, on a sheet of lightly floured parchment paper, roll out the dough into a circle. Slide the paper and dough onto a standard baking sheet. Spread the almond mixture over the dough, leaving an inch around the circumference. Now spread the cherries across the almonds, then fold the edges of the dough up to form a thicker edge to hold everything in. It'll look rustic—and that's the point. Before you stick the crostata in the oven, sprinkle the remaining tablespoon of sugar over the cherries and brush the edges of the pastry with melted butter. Bake for 1 hour or until browned.

SUNDAY

SUNDAY
29

EGG SANDWICHES

For people who worry about such things, there's fierce debate about when and where the breakfast sandwich was invented. Was it in the American South, with a fried egg between two biscuits? Was it the egg between two slices of toast (i.e., the staple of English diets for hundreds of years), or the open-faced rye bread version, with liverwurst or jams, preferred by Scandinavians? My go-to is the version you find all over New York, ideally from a cart on the street: the bacon, egg, and cheese, wrapped in wax paper and foil and ready to go.

There's zero debate about who invented the most universally popular breakfast sandwich in the U.S. and almost every other corner of the world. In 1971, Herb Peterson, an advertising exec and the owner of six McDonald's franchises in California, created the Egg McMuffin. He pitched it to McDonald's company owner Ray Kroc as a sure way to get customers in the door before noon. Kroc bit. (In fact, the story is that he polished off two Egg McMuffins at that meeting, he liked them so much.)

The Egg McMuffin isn't merely another breakfast sandwich. There's much more to it. Much more! Peterson was a clever guy. Instead of sliding

127

any misshapen fried egg into a buttered muffin, he invented an egg technique. It takes four steps: the McDonald's cook cracks eggs into individual Teflon rings, breaks each yolk with a spoon (to speed up and even out the cooking), sprays the tops of the eggs with a mist of water, and covers each one with a lid for a couple of minutes. The eggs are simultaneously fried and steamed on the hot top and come out of the Teflon rings as perfectly round pucks that fit neatly between the muffin halves.

It's that half-fried, half-steamed consistency that explains what makes the Egg McMuffin so different from other breakfast sandwiches. Combine that with oozing cheese and the saltiness of a round of bacon . . . and it's easy to polish off two or more. Another secret: you can order the McDonald's "round egg" as an add-on. Some people get it added to a Big Mac or a McChicken—whatever you want. Because every sandwich wants to be a breakfast sandwich.

What follows is my home hack version. You'll need a set of silicone baking rings or well-buttered round cookie cutters. They're worth the investment.

SERVES 2 TO 4

· ·

2 tablespoons vegetable oil, divided

4 slices bacon rounds

1 spray can cooking oil

4 large eggs

Salt and pepper to taste

4 English muffins, pried open with a fork

4 slices processed cheese

· ·

In a large skillet over medium-high heat, heat 1 tablespoon oil. Fry the bacon until crispy, then set aside on a plate with a sheet of paper towel to soak up the excess grease.

Wipe the skillet down and return to the cooktop, add the remaining 1 tablespoon oil, and lower the heat to medium. Spray four 3-inch cookie cutters or silicone baking rings with flavourless oil and place on the skillet. Crack the eggs and deposit one in each cutter, breaking the yolks with the back of a spoon. Sprinkle with salt and pepper. Mist the top of the eggs with water (I use a plant spray bottle), then place a 9-inch non-stick cake pan directly on the tops of the cutters and cook for 3 to 4 minutes, until the eggs are set. Meanwhile, toast the muffins.

Assemble the breakfast sandwiches by layering cheese, then eggs, then bacon (a second slice of cheese for the top doesn't hurt) on the toasted muffins. Season to taste. Eat immediately.

NO-WAFFLE-IRON WAFFLES

There's at least one kitchen gadget I've zero interest in owning: the waffle iron. I'd happily eat waffles for breakfast, lunch, and dinner (plus for elevenses, plus as an afternoon snack) but for the hassle of a waffle iron. People have been making waffles for eons (the ancient Greeks had their own flatter version called an obelios). An American with the splendid name of Cornelius Swartwout received a patent on August 24, 1869, for the first mass-manufactured waffle iron, a heavy panini-press-type contraption that you held over a coal- or wood-burning oven. The presses made today may be electric-powered, with built-in timers and variable settings, but they follow the same basic design. And despite the advent of non-stick surfaces and the like, they all have the same flaw: at some point, no matter how often you grease the iron's surface, the waffles burn and stick.

My Sam will also happily eat waffles for breakfast, lunch, and dinner. That's why we have a freezer full of Eggos, for any urgent waffle emergencies. He'll patiently watch the syrup pool in the waffle's divots, pointing out any that we miss, and then steadily munch his way from square to square. His love for waffles meant I had to find a way to make them without putting up with an actual waffle iron. Then I heard about a waffle shortcut touted by that master of shortcuts, Jamie Oliver.

Instead of a waffle iron, he uses a grilling pan. I already had one, which I use for grilling meats, whole peppers, and asparagus on my stovetop, especially on wet or wintry days when the BBQ isn't available. Mine is a square, 10-inch Le Creuset pan with a hard enamel cooking surface, which, at the right hot temperature, means food sears but never, ever sticks. Would it work for waffles? It was worth a try. I heated the pan to medium-low, brushed butter across the grills and into the crevices, crossed my fingers, and poured in the batter. Five minutes later, I tried slipping a spatula underneath to flip the waffle like an over-easy egg. It lifted clear off! And so did the next four waffles. I was impressed, and so was Sam's tummy.

If you already have a waffle iron, good for you. This recipe will work well no matter your cooking implement of choice. It also works just as well as a pancake batter should you not be in a waffle mood. And if the day happens to be August 24, you'd have a good excuse: the date that Swartwout received his patent is now known as National Waffle Day.

P.S. Any size grilling pan will work, as long as it has a high ridge around the edge to keep in the batter, but a smaller pan makes for easier flipping and lifting of the waffle.

SERVES 4 TO 6

• •

½ cup unsalted butter, plus more for buttering the pan and serving

3 cups all-purpose flour

½ cup whole wheat flour

5 tablespoons light brown sugar

1 tablespoon baking soda

1 teaspoon salt

4 eggs

4 cups whole milk

Maple syrup, for serving (optional)

1 cup whipped cream, for serving (optional)

• •

Melt the ½ cup butter in a mug in the microwave, and set aside to cool.

In a large mixing bowl with a spout, whisk together the all-purpose flour, whole wheat flour, sugar, baking soda, and salt. Using another set of medium mixing bowls, crack and separate the eggs. Using a hand mixer with the whisk attachment, whip the whites until they form frothy peaks, then set aside. To the bowl with the egg yolks, mix in the milk and melted butter. Tip that mixture in with the dry ingredients, stirring until just combined. Then carefully fold in the egg whites—you want to keep as much of their volume as you can.

Heat your grilling pan to medium-low. Melt a pat of butter, making sure it coats all the grooves. Pour in a cup of batter, tilting the pan so it spreads out evenly. Flip with a spatula after about 5 minutes, or when the surface is covered with small bubbles and seems to be getting drier. Grill the other side for another 5 minutes, then remove and serve with more butter, maple syrup, or whipped cream (or all three).

CHEDDAR POLENTA CAKES AND
BROWN SUGAR BACON

On the comfort scale, polenta makes a close rival to a steaming bowl of porridge or cream of wheat. It's nursery food—i.e., stuff for babies or for babying an adult. But when it cools, it turns into a savoury cake that would please even the most demanding queen (real or self-appointed). Like grits, polenta is infinitely better with the addition of cheese, cheese, and more cheese. Sometimes I'll grate in a gruyere or parmesan, but for breakfast I'll use a sharp, aged cheddar and briefly fry slices of the firmed-up polenta on a skillet. You could skip the first part of the cooking process and instead buy premade polenta from a supermarket—it usually comes in a tube, ready for slicing—but then you miss out on incorporating the cheese into the polenta. Plus, the consistency is always better when I make it from scratch.

Sam was initially skeptical about a yellow cake until I poured the mixture into muffin tins to cool. Polenta cupcakes! For sure he was into that. Even better, we serve them with brown sugar-jolted bacon. If we're extra hungry, fried eggs complete the savoury-sweet-salty picture.

SERVES 4

• •

For the polenta

4 cups low-sodium chicken broth

1 teaspoon salt

1 cup polenta (medium- or coarse-ground cornmeal)

1 teaspoon pepper

2 tablespoons butter

½ cup grated cheddar

¼ cup chopped Italian parsley, divided (optional)

For the bacon

1 pound bacon (about 16 slices)

½ cup brown sugar

• •

Grease a 12-cup muffin tin. In a medium saucepan, bring the broth to a boil. Add the salt and whisk in the polenta. Simmer on low for 5 minutes, whisking frequently to get rid of any lumps. Once it forms a smooth paste, cover the pot and simmer for half an hour. Give the polenta a vigorous stir with a wooden spoon every 5 minutes. When the polenta is almost too thick to stir, take off the heat. Mix in pepper, butter, cheese, and half the chopped parsley.

Spoon the mixture into the prepared muffin tins. Let cool, uncovered, in the fridge for 2 hours or, ideally, overnight. Before serving, sprinkle the reserved parsley overtop.

To make the bacon, preheat the oven to 425°F. Place an oven-safe metal wire rack on top of parchment paper in a baking sheet. Spread out the bacon evenly on the rack. Distribute the sugar over the bacon. Bake for 10 to 15 minutes or until browned and mostly crispy, depending on the thickness of your bacon. This can be made ahead and served at room temperature.

BREAKFAST BURRITOS

When I'm anxious that I'm letting Sam watch too many videos of surprised cat reactions on YouTube, I remember how I spent every Saturday morning of my childhood watching *He-Man* and *Scooby-Doo*. Growing up near the Canada–U.S. border, I knew all the names of the Buffalo weather reporters, the jingles for their accident attorneys and used auto lots, and whatever the latest 99-cent deal was at the American fast-food chains. The most tempting commercials were for frozen breakfast burritos. Mom would make us Old El Paso tacos at least once a week, but I was amazed to hear you could also have burritos in the morning—and that kids in the U.S. were working miracles by microwaving them in three minutes flat.

Now the supermarket near me has a dozen options for burritos, breakfast and regular format, in the freezer section, and most breakfast restaurants and diners serve them too, even if they call them breakfast wraps. At home we make a speedy version for when we're late getting out the door. Our recipe uses store-bought large tortilla wraps, and if you want to skip the step of peeling, boiling, and frying potatoes, you can sub in a package of frozen hash browns. Sam likes that this goes quickly, as it means we get a little more time to watch cartoons before we start with our schedule of chores and errands and visits with relatives. His favourite cartoon of the moment is the unavoidable *PAW Patrol*. When he's a bit older, I'll introduce him to *Scooby-Doo*.

SERVES 4

• •

4 large tortilla wraps

1 pound bacon (about 16 slices)

2 large potatoes, peeled and diced, or ½ pound frozen hash browns

Butter, for frying

4 eggs

1 cup grated aged cheddar or Monterey Jack

Pepper

Handful of ripe cherry tomatoes, diced

1 ripe avocado, peeled, pitted, and diced

Crema or sour cream to taste

• •

In a skillet over medium-high heat, warm the wraps one at a time, flipping partway through—about 3 to 4 minutes each. Place the warmed wraps between two clean tea towels until ready to assemble.

At the same time, in another skillet over medium-high heat, cook the bacon until crisp. Set the bacon aside on a couple of sheets of paper towel. Once cooled, crumble into bite-size pieces. Make sure to reserve the bacon fat in the pan.

If you're using the diced potatoes, boil them in a medium pot of water until tender enough that a fork will easily pierce a piece, but not so soft that they dissolve on contact. Drain and fry them in the skillet with the bacon fat until they're charred and crisp, about 10 minutes. If you're using the frozen hash browns, skip the boiling step and go straight to frying.

In the skillet you used for the burrito wraps, melt the butter and scramble the eggs. Just before they're done, sprinkle the cheese overtop and season with some fresh-ground pepper. Combine and remove from the heat.

Now you're ready to assemble the burritos. This can be the part of the recipe for a kid to master. Down the centre of each wrap, layer a few spoonfuls of the potatoes, eggs, and tomatoes, leaving a good inch from the top and bottom clear for folding. To taste, add the crumbled bacon, some diced avocado, and a drizzle of crema. Fold over one of the sides of burrito. Turn up the bottom and the top of the wrap by an inch, then fold over the other side until you form a rectangular pillow. Serve immediately.

CROISSANT CROQUE MADAME

Some day, when we have extra time, we'll challenge ourselves with homemade croissants. It's a major project, between the folding and chilling of the dough, over and over, until you get what pro bakers call 100 percent lamination. If you don't put in all that work—and waiting— a croissant won't puff up or leave the oven with a crisp, flaky outside and a buttery, fibrous middle. They're very satisfying to make on your own, a much bigger coup than another loaf of sourdough.

For now, we're very happy with the croissants from a Parisian-style patisserie around the block from us. On Saturday I'll make a point of buying more than I need, because I want to have at least three or four left over for Sunday morning. The secret usefulness of the day-old croissant is something I learned in the late 1990s, when I was a student in Montreal. I spent many idle mornings with university friends in a neighbourhood bistro with a black and white tile floor and newspapers on reading sticks. We'd order croque monsieur because it was the cheapest thing on the menu, or croque madame if we were feeling ready to splurge on an egg. Most days the only bread options for the sandwich were a crusty white or rye. Sometimes, without you asking, the kitchen would make your sandwich on a croissant.

Montrealers are nearly as particular about their croissants as they are about their bagels, and the best ones came from a Belgian patisserie where you filled your own paper bag from racks where the croissants were cooling down. I was impressed that the bistro's cooks were able to fry the croissant without it shattering or generally turning into a sloppy mess (they didn't hold back on the butter in the pan). Then one friend, a born Montrealer, explained that they'd certainly be using day-olds. Day-old croissants are both softer and tougher than their freshly baked counterparts. Using slightly stale croissants for a croque monsieur or croque madame is the same principle as using a day-old baguette or loaf of challah for French toast. It's a way to make sure no bread goes to waste, but the recipe is also counting on the hardier integrity of the bread's staleness.

SERVES 4

· ·

4 day-old croissants

4 slices emmental or brie

4 slices Black Forest ham

Small bunch chives, finely sliced (optional)

Butter, for frying

4 eggs

· ·

Preheat the oven to 275°F.

Slice the croissants in half and slice each cheese and ham piece into two obtuse triangles. In between each piece of croissant, layer the ham and cheese (each croissant will get two triangles of cheese and two triangles of ham). Add a sprinkle of chives, saving some for a garnish.

In a large skillet over medium-high heat, melt the butter. Fry the sandwiches, croissant base down, for 5 minutes or until the cheese has melted. Depending on the size of your pan, you may need to do this in batches. You'll only fry the one side. Place the fried sandwiches on a baking sheet in the oven to keep warm. Now fry the eggs, sunny-side up. Top each sandwich with a fried egg and a sprinkle of chives.

WIENERS AND BEANS

My mom was of a North American generation for which it was still not uncommon for a woman to give up work to raise the kids. When she met my dad, she was a dental hygienist, which was what she slid into after university. Even when she was at her happiest, she always seemed to be drifting away, looking for something better. In between driving us kids to hockey practice, she found creative outlets: watercolours, decoupage (a table in the basement was always threatening to tip over with a Mod Podge bottle), weaving, gardening, and sewing our Halloween costumes. Once a week, she'd try an elaborate new recipe out of her cookbook collection. At the end of dinner my dad would always ask if tomorrow she'd make roast beef and potatoes, or just pasta and sauce—something ordinary. But I liked the exotic dinners, or at least as a preteen I liked the idea that there was something more interesting to life than the meat and potatoes of our small suburban city.

When Mom needed something quick to feed us for lunch, and sometimes for dinner, she'd fill a pot with a can of Heinz baked beans and two or three sliced-up hotdogs, and heat them until the sauce gave off a faintly caramelly scent and the hotdog ends burst open. In university, I seemed to crave wieners and beans during exams or if I had an overdue essay. Wieners and beans took me back to the glossy oak table in my parents' kitchen. A bowl of wieners and beans was like wrapping myself in a security blanket. Today, on the rare night or weekend that I'm home alone and left to my devices, I'll start searching for the can opener. I sometimes don't bother ladling the cooked wieners and beans into a bowl, and instead eat them straight from the pot while leaning against the stove, like a solitary camper in the woods.

While I'll never turn down ready-made baked beans, they taste even better if you bake them yourself. One of the easiest methods is to use a slow cooker, but it has the drawback of taking the entire day, especially if you're starting with dried beans. In the winter I'll cook baked beans and sausages for a hearty weekend brunch, usually with a plate of fried eggs and a loaf of crusty bread. (However much I'd like to, I'd never get away with serving hot dogs for breakfast.) To speed things up, I've been improvising on a shortcut cassoulet recipe by the chef and cooking school instructor Michael Olson, who once ran a winery restaurant near my hometown. Cassoulet is the French version of wieners and beans. It's also a notoriously slow and involved recipe—if you're doing it right, it takes a full two days! Olson cuts two days down to two hours by using canned beans instead of dried. And instead of preparing the traditional duck confit, he starts by frying bacon with slices of garlicky sausage, which helps build a meaty flavour into the beans. The final result approximates the richness of wieners and beans, but is far less sugary.

SERVES 6

• •

2 cans (each 19 ounces) white kidney beans or 30 ounces dried

½ pound French country sausages, sliced into 1-inch pieces

6 slices bacon, cut into 1-inch pieces

1 yellow onion, diced

2 stalks celery, diced

2 carrots, peeled and diced

1 teaspoon dried oregano

1 teaspoon chopped fresh thyme

1 clove garlic, crushed

1 (16-ounce) can whole roma tomatoes

2 cups chicken broth

2 tablespoons Worcestershire sauce

½ cup dry bread crumbs

4 tablespoons butter, divided

6 eggs, for frying

1 loaf crusty bread, for serving

• •

If you're using canned beans, rinse them and set aside. If using dried, soak them overnight in a bowl under a few inches of water.

Preheat the oven to 350°F.

Heat a 5-quart Dutch oven to medium-high. Once hot, fry the sausages and bacon, stirring occasionally, until the bacon has rendered and the sausages are browned. Add the onions, celery, carrots, oregano, thyme, and garlic and sauté until tender—about 5 minutes.

Crush the tomatoes in the can with your hand, then pour into the Dutch oven along with the beans, broth, and Worcestershire sauce. Stir until evenly combined. Distribute the bread crumbs evenly on top, then break up 3 tablespoons butter and place a piece here and there. Bake, uncovered, in the oven for 2 hours.

When breakfast hour arrives, melt the reserved butter in a medium-high skillet and fry the eggs to your desired doneness. Serve bowls of the wieners and beans with an egg on top and a slice of crusty bread on the side.

BANANA BREAD WITH
BRANDY BUTTER ICING

There are Sundays when the usual breakfast staples—eggs, meat, griddled this and that—just aren't appealing. Or when you've got people coming over who don't eat meat or object to the scent of cooking eggs, or are otherwise impossible to please. In those circumstances, it's good to have a backup. That backup should be banana bread. Even the lightest banana breads are heftier and more filling than most other baked goods. Add some icing (our household is fond of a butter icing with a touch of brandy) and serve it with a big bowl of fruit salad or fresh berries, plus a fresh pot of coffee, and you're set.

It goes without saying that you can't make banana bread unless you've got ripe bananas, so for all my talk of a "backup," this recipe still requires some forethought. It's also heavy on the bananas—four, compared to the typical two- or three-banana loaf—and is best made in a Bundt pan. So, if we're being strict about it, this is technically a cake, but so is any "bread" that you make by creaming sugar and butter. Nuts are optional, but if your visitors aren't allergic, I recommend mixing some chopped toasted pecans into the batter and then, after you've iced the top of the cake (bread!), placing a half-dozen pecan halves on top. The nuts say, "Hey, I made some effort, and pay attention because this isn't your average banana bread."

SERVES 8 TO 10

• •

For the banana bread

2⅓ cups all-purpose flour

¾ cup granulated sugar

1 teaspoon baking powder

1 teaspoon baking soda

¾ teaspoon salt

4 ripe bananas

3 eggs, separated into yolks and whites

½ cup milk

½ cup canola oil

1 teaspoon vanilla paste

½ cup chopped and toasted pecans (optional)

For the brandy butter icing

½ cup plus 2 tablespoons unsalted butter

1½ cups powdered sugar

2 tablespoons brandy

12 pecan halves, for topping (optional)

• •

Preheat the oven to 350°F. Butter every nook and cranny of the inside of a Bundt pan, then dust with flour to help prevent the cake from sticking.

In a large mixing bowl, whisk together the flour, sugar, baking powder, baking soda, and salt. In a medium bowl, mash the bananas with a fork, then mix well with the egg yolks, milk, oil, and vanilla. Pour into the dry mixture and mix until just combined. If you're including the nuts, stir them into the batter. Now, in a dry mixing bowl, whisk the egg whites until they turn solid white and form peaks. This will take some extra muscle, and you may want to take turns with an eager kid. Alternatively, use an electric mixer, which will later come in handy if you're making the brandy butter.

Fold the whites into the batter, being careful not to overmix (you want to keep that extra volume from the whites). Pour the batter into the pan and bake for 45 minutes. Test by inserting a toothpick or wood skewer into the cake—if it comes out clean, it's done.

While the cake is cooling, make the brandy butter icing. It's simple: in a medium mixing bowl, cream the butter and then add the powdered sugar, trying your best to avoid it blowing everywhere. Mix until smooth, then add the brandy to taste. You'll have enough icing to spread over the very top of the cooled cake—any more would be too rich, especially at breakfast. Decorate the top with pecan halves.

DIY POP-TARTS

Jam-filled mini pies were around long before 1964, when Kellogg's introduced Pop-Tarts. But the Pop-Tart has the advantage of needing no refrigeration. They just sit there, in your cupboard, keeping "fresh" for an eternity. That's one reason why they're every college student's favourite exam prep snack. And why the U.S. military air-dropped two million of them on unsuspecting Afghans during the 2001 invasion. Bodybuilders are known to carry boxes in their workout bags for when they require an instant surge of carbs. Pop-Tarts can also be dangerous. In 1994 a Texas A&M University-Corpus Christi instructor with too much time on his hands conducted an experiment in which he demonstrated that an unfrosted strawberry Pop-Tart left a few minutes too long in a toaster, on high, will catch fire. Two-foot-high flames shot out.

Are Pop-Tarts good for your overall health? Definitely not. But they're dependably good, sometimes even incredibly good. Since the 1980s the product developers at Kellogg's started supplementing the original strawberry jam and fudge version of Pop-Tarts with specialized fillings and toppings that say a lot about their era, and about the evolving tastes of kids: Frosted S'Mores (amazingly close to the campfire classic), Dulce de Leche (a full-on burnt-sugar rush), Gone Nutty! Frosted Chocolate Peanut Butter (like an amped-up Reese's cup), Frosted Spidey-Berry (one of many superhero tie-ins), Splitz Drizzled Sugar Cookie/Frosted Brownie Batter (one of many Pop-Tarts with "splitz" flavours, in this case sugar cookie on one side and chocolaty batter on the other), Frosted Sparkle-Licious Cherry (one of many recent sparkled pastries targeted at rainbow unicorns and their fans), Indiana Jones Frosted Brown Sugar Cinnamon (more appetizing than eyeball soup, but not clear on what the candy heart flavour has to do with swashbuckling archaeology), and Choc-o-Lantern Frosted Chocolate Fudge (a seasonal variety that has a fudge filling, pumpkin-orange frosting, and sprinkles shaped like ghosts and bats). And on and on. There are at least 50 varieties, most of them discontinued, and an entire underground network of collectors who chase after a complete set.

If you're poking around online, you'll find a cottage industry of home bakers who share recipes on how to make your own. The fillings are relatively easy to recreate, and so are the various icing flavours, but everyone struggles to replicate the peculiarly dry and grainy texture and taste of Pop-Tart pastry, which is the secret to how the store-bought version holds its shape in the box and in the toaster oven. The dry pastry is my least favourite part of a factory-made Pop-Tart. To make them at home, I use the same butter and lard recipe I prefer for pie crusts, which never fails me and creates a pastry that's buttery and always flaky, even if I make the mistake of kneading it too long or adding too much moisture. If you haven't planned ahead (the pastry dough requires chilling), you can instead use a defrosted store-bought pie crust. For the filling I usually make a quick jam with whatever berries are in the fridge, but a nice-quality store-bought jam will do just fine.

MAKES 8 TO 10 TARTS

● ●

For the pastry

2½ cups all-purpose flour

1 teaspoon salt

1 teaspoon granulated sugar

1 cup lard

8 tablespoons unsalted butter

½ cup ice water

For the filling

2 cups berries (if using strawberries, hull and chop into eighths)

1 cup granulated sugar

1 tablespoon lemon juice

Zest of 1 lemon

For the icing

1 cup powdered sugar

2 tablespoons whipping cream

1 teaspoon vanilla paste

To assemble

All-purpose flour, for rolling

1 egg

1 tablespoon water

● ●

Start by making the pastry. In a food processor with a pastry blade, mix the flour, salt, and sugar. Cut the lard and butter into 1-inch pieces, then pulse into the flour mixture until it starts to resemble coarse sand. Stop immediately. In stages, slowly drizzle in the ice water and pulse the mixture. Once it starts to cohere, stop mixing. Gather the dough into a ball, divide in half, wrap each half in plastic wrap, and chill in the fridge for at least half an hour.

While the dough is chilling, place all the berries, granulated sugar, lemon juice, and lemon zest in a small saucepan and cook on medium-low heat, stirring occasionally, until the berries have collapsed and formed a thick sauce, about 10 to 12 minutes. Set aside to cool.

For the icing, whisk together the powdered sugar, cream, and vanilla paste in a measuring cup with a spout. It's ready when it's smooth and glossy. Cover and set aside.

Preheat the oven to 425°F. Line a baking sheet with parchment paper.

Now it's time to start the assembly process. Flour a clean kitchen surface. Working with one ball of dough at a time, roll out the dough on the floured surface into a rough rectangular shape about ¼ inch thick. Cut out smaller rectangles (aim for 3 × 4 inches), then use a spatula to lift and place on the prepared baking sheet, allowing for an inch or so between each rectangle. These will serve as the base of your tarts. Roll out the second ball of dough, adding more flour to your surface if needed, and repeat creating rectangles—these are your tops.

Spoon 2 teaspoons of the filling into the middle of each base rectangle. Mix the egg and water in a small bowl, and brush the edges of each rectangle base with the egg wash. Carefully place the top rectangles onto the bases. Brush the tops with the remaining egg wash, then use a fork to crimp around all their edges, forming a seal. Bake for 20 minutes. They're ready when they're golden brown—don't let them get too dark.

Wait for them to cool completely. This will take some patience, but it's worth it. Then drizzle the icing onto each tart's top, spreading to the edges with the back of a spoon. You could wait a few minutes to let the icing set, or you could just as easily eat them straightaway. No toaster required. Leftovers will keep for 2 to 3 days in an airtight container.

PUMPKIN SPICE PANCAKES

There's enough pumpkin spice in our world, between lattes and doughnuts and scented candles. What was once a seasonal treat is now a year-round fact of life. At the risk of instigating a jack o'lantern apocalypse, I'd like to argue that every pancake should be pumpkin-spiced too. Okay, not every single pancake. But if you have a can of unsweetened pumpkin purée kicking around, there's no harm mixing it into your batter. In fact, it'll add another layer of sweetness and ensure your pancakes don't dry out. They'll have a faint orangey hue, which makes them an appropriate Sunday treat for kids come Halloween, or really any time.

SERVES 4

• •

1½ cups all-purpose flour

¼ cup granulated sugar

1½ teaspoons baking powder

½ teaspoon baking soda

½ teaspoon salt

½ teaspoon cinnamon

¼ teaspoon nutmeg

¼ teaspoon ground cloves

¼ teaspoon ground ginger

1½ cups buttermilk

¼ cup unsalted butter, melted

2 eggs

½ cup unsweetened pumpkin purée

½ teaspoon lemon zest

Butter, for frying

1 tablespoon powdered sugar

1 cup whipping cream

• •

In a large mixing bowl (with a spout, if available), combine the flour, sugar, baking powder, baking soda, salt, cinnamon, nutmeg, cloves, and ginger. In a separate medium mixing bowl, whisk the buttermilk, melted butter, eggs, pumpkin, and lemon zest until smooth. Stir the wet ingredients into the dry until just combined. Leave the uncovered batter in the fridge for a minimum of half an hour to help the ingredients mellow.

In a skillet over medium heat, melt the butter. Working in batches, ladle ¼ cup of batter for each pancake. Flip them when the tops are covered in small bubbles and beginning to look drier. After a minute, remove from the pan. This recipe makes around 12 to 18 pancakes.

While the pancakes are cooking, whisk the powdered sugar and cream in the cleaned medium bowl until gentle peaks form. Spoon the whipped cream onto each stack of pancakes.

GREEN EGGS AND HAM

One of the first storybooks Sam latched onto was Dr. Seuss's *Green Eggs and Ham*. That had to be inevitable, given the name of the book's breakfast-pushing antagonist. And like anyone who encounters that book, he was floored by the idea that breakfast could be green. So it was also inevitable that we'd make green eggs and ham for our next Sunday recipe challenge. Most of the home-cook tips for preparing green eggs involve food colouring (blue does the trick for yellow yolks), but I decided to go the all-natural spinach route. I also figured it'd be an interesting experiment to make it all on one baking sheet, a variation on a frittata.

The main selling feature for one-sheet recipes is just that—everything cooks on one sheet, so there's only that one thing to clean up. That under-sells the other, even greater superpower of one-sheet recipes, which is how the flavours of whatever you're roasting or baking together will meld. It's the same magic principle behind casseroles, lasagna, and shakshuka.

One sheet doesn't always mean fast. In this case, the cooking is done in stages. The baby potatoes get roasted first, then the vegetables are added, and then the ham and eggs. Because the eggs have been through a blender (oops, I should mention there's a blender involved—this is one sheet plus a blender), you'll need to use a baking sheet with a rim at least an inch high to prevent the whole thing pouring into your oven. If you don't have one, a rectangular cake or brownie pan would also work—or even an extra-large cast-iron skillet.

SERVES 6

● ●

1 pound baby potatoes, halved

4 tablespoons olive oil, divided

2 teaspoons salt, divided

2 teaspoons pepper, divided

1 green zucchini, sliced into ½-inch pieces

12 cherry tomatoes, halved

12 eggs

2½ cups baby spinach

Small bunch Italian parsley, plus more for garnish

¼ cup whipping cream

½ cup freshly grated parmesan

1 cup cubed Black Forest ham

● ●

Preheat the oven to 425°F.

In a large bowl, toss the potatoes in 2 tablespoons olive oil and 1 teaspoon each of salt and pepper, then spread out on a baking sheet. Roast in the oven for half an hour. In the same bowl, toss the zucchini and tomatoes in the remaining 2 tablespoons oil and 1 teaspoon each of salt and pepper. Add to the pan and roast for another 20 minutes.

~~→

While the vegetables are roasting, crack the eggs into a blender. Add the spinach, parsley, cream, and parmesan. Blend until smooth. Add the egg mixture to the baking sheet, tilting the pan carefully from side to side until the eggs have spread to every corner (it helps to wear extra-thick oven mitts for this). Distribute the cubes of ham around the pan. Return the pan to the oven, lower the heat to 375°F, and bake for 10 minutes or until the eggs are set.

Let the pan rest outside the oven for 5 minutes, then place in the middle of the table (the pan will still be hot, so don't forget to use a couple of trivets), and garnish with a few last parsley leaves across the top.

SALMON AND EGG SANDWICHES

In my experience, half the population can't get enough pink fish and the other half can't get far enough away. It's not that pink fish are necessarily more "fishy" tasting (white fish like cod are among the fishiest). Instead, it's more about the special texture of pink fish, which are chewier and would never be described (unlike, say, a fillet of Icelandic cod) as "buttery."

I'm in the first camp, especially when it comes to smoked salmon, but Sam and Stephen are definitely in the second. My usual tactic to convince Sam to eat stuff is to smother it in tomato sauce. That doesn't work as well with salmon. Then I landed on another trick: disguise it twice over. If the smoked salmon is diced small enough, combined with eggs and cream, and then hidden in a bun, he'll eat it. Maybe it's the bun that's working in my favour. I usually make this recipe for us using soft potato buns—the same kind that are now standard at indie burger shops. Potato buns, like potato bread, are made with a mix of regular and potato flour, and it's the latter that keeps the buns moist, something like a butter-enriched brioche bun. Speaking of which, if you swap in brioche buns or a fresh croissant instead of a potato bun, no worries. But now that

I've figured out that Sam will eat this if there's a potato bun involved, I don't want to jinx it.

SERVES 4

• •

4 potato buns, sliced in half

Butter, for frying

6 eggs

½ cup whipping cream

Salt and pepper to taste

8 to 10 ounces smoked salmon, cut into bite-size pieces

• •

Heat a skillet to medium-high. Butter the insides of each bun half and, in batches, grill facing down in the hot skillet. Set aside.

In a mixing bowl, whisk the eggs together with the cream. Season with salt and pepper. Melt a pat of butter in the skillet, coating the surface, and then pour in the egg mixture. Stir the eggs as they cook. As they start to firm up, mix in the salmon. Stir until the eggs are just set. If the eggs are too firm, add more butter and quickly stir to combine. Divide the eggs between the four bun bases, grind a little more pepper on each, then add the top bun and you're all set.

MINI MONKEY BREAD

Rolled balls of dough in butter, sugar, and cinnamon smushed tight into a
Bundt pan—in the baking world, monkey bread isn't all that unique. It's
a simplified version of a Hungarian coffee cake and a Polish babka, and a
close relative of the cinnamon roll. Its name is also an instruction: much
like a monkey would, you pull the chunks of baked bread apart by hand.
I like everything about monkey bread except for how some sections of the
dough, especially those buried in the middle of the Bundt pan, always seem
too raw unless you leave it to bake too long and risk drying out the rest.

My solution, by no means an original one, is nevertheless foolproof:
bake the balls of sugar-coated dough in muffin tins. You get a more even
bake and no dry spots. Because it's a yeast dough, the bread takes some
preparation to allow the dough to rise (you can also make the dough
the night before, as long as you let it come to room temperature before
shaping it the next morning). This muffin tin shortcut also has the
advantage of shortening the baking time, which is important when
your house is jumping with hungry little monkeys.

MAKES 1 DOZEN MINI MONKEY BREADS

. . . .

For the dough

1½ cups milk

1 package active dry yeast (about 2 teaspoons)

¼ cup granulated sugar

⅓ cup butter, melted

2 eggs

1 teaspoon salt

5 cups all-purpose flour

For the coating

¾ cup unsalted butter, melted

1 cup granulated sugar

1 cup packed light brown sugar

1½ tablespoons cinnamon

1 cup powdered sugar

2 tablespoons milk

1 teaspoon vanilla paste

. . . .

In a small saucepan over medium heat, warm the milk to 110°F. You'll need a kitchen thermometer to keep an eye on the temp. Mix the yeast, milk, and sugar in the bowl of a stand mixer until dissolved, then cover and let rest for a good 10 minutes. Now add the butter, eggs, and salt. Beat on low speed until combined. At this point, replace the mixer's paddle with a dough hook. Gradually add the flour, cup by cup, and beat until it forms a dough, then increase the speed and knead for another couple of minutes. Now place the ball of dough in a bowl lightly coated with oil. Cover and let rest in a warm spot for a couple of hours, or until the dough doubles in size.

In a bowl, mix the butter, granulated sugar, brown sugar, and cinnamon. Divide into two bowls, setting one aside.

Grease a 12-cup muffin tin with butter. Once the dough has risen, punch it down to release its air, then pull off pieces and roll into balls. You should aim for 36 balls in total. Roll each ball in the butter and sugar mixture until well coated. Place three balls into each cup of the muffin tin—though if you end up with four or five smaller balls, it's all good. Once they're all filled, cover the tray with plastic wrap and set aside to let rest for half an hour. They'll rise again, doubling in size.

Preheat the oven to 350°F.

Uncover the monkey balls and spoon the remaining butter-sugar mixture over each. Bake for 20 minutes or until they're golden brown. Keep an eye on them—a moment too long and the sugar burns. If you feel like some extra icing to drizzle on top, whisk together a bowl of the powdered sugar, milk, and vanilla.

MAPLE SCONES

One winter morning, to break up a fight between me and my brother over
who got to control the remote, Mom announced that we were making
scones. Scones are one of the easiest things in the world to bake, but
Mom went one step easier: she used Betty Crocker Bisquick mix. Biscuits
and scones aren't that different. Biscuits, which I knew about from PBS
cooking shows, are American and typically more buttery. Scones are more
common in Canada—I guess because so many of our recipes came from
the U.K., but also because scones are known for being powdery and dry,
and between our long winters and our notorious politeness, so are we.

It wasn't until the late 1990s that scones started to get more interesting
than plain or plain with butter. Bakeries added cranberries and dried
fruit, coated them in icing, and generally converted what had been a dry
accompaniment to tea into a full-on dessert that you might want to eat
on its own.

Now I make scones at home with Sam, and we try to strike a balance
between a traditional scone and the sweeter versions. Our scones take
a cue from the ones served at the Rose Bakery, which is the strangest

thing: a great English-style bakery in the middle of Paris. Their scones get their special texture from the addition of steel-cut oats. I'm extra generous with the maple syrup, since it's easier to come by in Canada. It's also prudent to reserve more syrup to drizzle over the finished scones at the table. They're good with coffee or tea. Like a biscuit, they're just as good on a plate of eggs and breakfast sausage.

MAKES 2 DOZEN SCONES

• •

3 cups all-purpose flour

1 cup quick-cook steel-cut oats

2 tablespoons granulated sugar

2 tablespoons baking powder

1 teaspoon kosher salt

1½ cups unsalted butter, cut into ¼-inch pieces

3 large eggs

½ cup Grade A maple syrup, plus more for drizzling

½ cup milk

½ cup raisins (optional)

¼ cup candied orange peel (optional)

1 egg plus 1 tablespoon water, for egg wash

• •

Preheat the oven to 400°F. Line two baking sheets with parchment paper.

In a food processor, pulse the flour, oats, sugar, baking powder, and salt until combined. Add the butter and pulse until it resembles coarse sand. Mix in two of the eggs, the syrup, and the milk until they're just combined. Avoid overmixing; it should just come together.

Roll the dough onto a lightly floured counter. At this point, you'd knead in the optional raisins and the orange peel until evenly distributed. Roll out the dough until just over 1 inch thick. Using the rim of a lightly floured juice glass, cut out rounds, working the scraps of dough together when necessary.

Place the rounds an inch apart on the prepared baking sheets, then brush the tops with an egg wash to hasten browning. Bake one sheet at a time for 20 minutes, rotating halfway through. They're done when they've puffed up and the tops are golden brown. While still warm, drizzle with more syrup. Serve immediately. They'll keep for a day in an airtight container.

HAM AND SAGE FRITTATA

The first weekend I made us a frittata, Sam asked why I gave his omelette a silly name. My favourite omelettes are often plain, maybe with a small amount of cheese, but frittatas are what I make when we have leftover ham or sausage, or some other vegetables ready to be used up. The main difference between the two, in fact, is that frittatas tend to be larger and can serve two or more people, and therefore need to be cooked longer and over medium heat, while the typical omelette is cooked over a higher heat and made for one person.

The size of the frittata will often mean that it's easier to start cooking on a stovetop and finish in an oven, rather than flip over. And by often, I mean always. Any frittata containing more than five eggs (which is most of them) requires a strong resolve and a lot of luck to slide onto a plate and flip back into the pan without losing half of it on the burner or the floor.

The other distinguishing feature of a frittata is that the longer cooking time means the outside gets browned and crispier than an omelette, while the inside ideally remains soft even when fully set. That outer edge is especially delicious when bits of the ham or herb filling get pushed out and crisped up too. In our house, we usually have a small ham every other week or so, and there's always some left over. In Spain and Italy it's not uncommon to add chopped fresh sage, which has a grassier flavour than the powder variety, to ham and eggs. In the spring, sage is the second or third herb to pop up in our garden, after the chives and thyme. I originally planted the section of sage thinking I'd need plenty for lamb and poultry roasts, but it grows nearly as fast as parsley and I find myself giving it away to neighbours. I'll also fry whole sage leaves in olive oil and toss them on top of the finished frittata—or just have them by the handful, like chips. This recipe is a good excuse to pluck a few more leaves.

SERVES 4

• •

8 eggs

3 tablespoons milk or cream

1 cup diced Black Forest ham

2 tablespoons freshly grated parmesan

Pepper to taste

5 fresh sage leaves, finely chopped

Butter, for frying

4 slices toasted and buttered sourdough bread

• •

Preheat the oven to 350°F.

In a large mixing bowl, whisk the eggs and milk. Add the ham, parmesan, pepper, and sage and mix to combine.

In a large skillet over medium heat, melt the butter, then add the egg mixture. When the eggs are half set, transfer the pan to the oven. Bake

for 15 minutes or until the top is golden brown and springy to the touch.
Serve with buttered sourdough toast.

Variations: Replace the ham and sage with mixed cheeses (gruyere,
fontina, and parmesan go well together) or a vegetable (zucchini or
eggplant are ideal) that's been thinly sliced and fried in olive oil until
soft before being added to the frittata.

ORANGE CAKE

Not that long ago, it was possible to believe there were only two types of winter citrus: navel oranges and bitter white grapefruit. Then supermarkets started to import pink grapefruit, mandarins, and clementines, among others, and winters started to seem more bearable. When oranges are at their peak—around January, when the first Cara Cara and Jaffa oranges hit the shelves—I look for any excuse to cook or bake with them, adding oranges to roast chicken, to pan-fried brussels sprouts, and always to cakes.

This recipe started out as an apple-raisin cake, but replacing them with oranges makes it less snoozy. I'll usually use Cara Cara or plain navel oranges, though if the blood oranges are sweet, they'll work just as well. Adding ground almond meal to the flour keeps the baked cake extra moist. It also makes this a heavier cake—a *Great British Bake Off* judge would dismiss it as "stodgy"—which I like, especially on a snowy weekend. I'd recommend having some as a midafternoon snack, but I've never had the pleasure. It's always disappeared by noon.

SERVES 4 TO 6

• • • • • • • • • • • • • • • • • • • •

¾ cup unsalted butter	1 teaspoon vanilla paste
1¼ cups granulated sugar	1 cup all-purpose flour
3 eggs	1 cup almond meal
1 tablespoon orange zest	1 teaspoon baking powder
2 tablespoons orange juice	Pinch of salt

• • • • • • • • • • • • • • • • • • • •

Preheat the oven to 325°F. Line a 9-inch loaf pan with parchment paper by inserting one piece lengthwise and another across the middle, so the sheets cover all four sides.

In a stand mixer with the cake paddle, cream the butter and sugar until smooth. Add the eggs, one at a time, then the zest, juice, and vanilla. In a separate bowl, mix together the flour, almond meal, baking powder, and salt. Gradually tip the dry ingredients into the batter, mixing on a low speed until just combined—don't overmix.

Pour the batter into the prepared loaf pan. Bake for 1 hour or until a toothpick poked into the cake comes out clean. Cool on a rack. The cake will stay fresh for up to 2 days on the counter, loosely covered with plastic wrap.

TOUTONS AND BLUEBERRY JAM

One of my first trips to Cape Breton was for my father-in-law's 75th birthday, which meant a long weekend of beers on the back porch, a lobster boil, and enough butterscotch cream pies to keep all the grandkids happy. That trip, Sam wasn't yet a year old. We stayed at a hotel perched up on a rise. It was eerily big and quiet. The hotel had long, carpeted hallways, and a few times I spotted someone disappearing off in the distance—or at least I thought I did. It had a distinct Overlook Hotel in *The Shining* vibe.

Our first morning, we took our chances on the hotel restaurant. A pair of grandmotherly servers were rushing about delivering orders of tea and toast. Every table had a view of fishing boats in the harbour. Even though we were early, the breakfast buffet had been picked over, aside for a few trays of eggs and sausages and, over to one side, what appeared to be brown hockey pucks. Those, Stephen explained, are toutons. Tow-what? I asked. They're a fry bread, he said, and you usually have them with some syrup or molasses—molasses if you're following tradition. Just try them.

Toutons aren't easy to find outside of Newfoundland unless you're in Cape Breton, where they see a lot of traffic from the Newfoundland ferry. They're an easy way to use up leftover bread dough. Toutons should be served hot from the frying pan. Kids like them—they're a distant cousin of doughnuts, so what's not to like—especially with sweet molasses. It can seem like Newfoundlanders drizzle molasses on everything, but it makes extra sense with toutons, which in the standard recipes are fried in pork fat. The molasses' sweetness balances out the salty pork.

Making toutons back at home, I've opted to fry them in butter and oil, which makes less of a mess and is arguably healthier, and I serve them with fresh jam instead of molasses. That said, you should try them with molasses at least once, to get the full experience. I recommend blueberry jam, which I associate with the East Coast.

When we finally made it to my in-laws' house that morning, the party had already started and everyone was digging into a late breakfast. There were plates set aside for us. I was still so full from the hotel that I tried to excuse myself. Never mind, said Stephen's mom, why don't you try some of these? We call them toutons.

MAKES 2 DOZEN TOUTONS AND 2 CUPS JAM

• • • • • • • • • • • • • • • • • • • •

For the toutons

1½ cups milk

1 package active dry yeast (about 2 teaspoons)

¼ cup granulated sugar

2 tablespoons shortening

1 teaspoon salt

5 cups all-purpose flour

⅓ cup vegetable oil, plus more for oiling the bowl

3 tablespoons butter, plus more for serving with the toutons

For the jam

2 cups wild blueberries

½ cup honey or granulated sugar

1 tablespoon lemon juice

• • • • • • • • • • • • • • • • • • • •

⟿➤

Start by preparing the dough. In a small saucepan over medium heat, warm the milk to 110°F (you'll need a kitchen thermometer to make sure you get it just right). In the bowl of a stand mixer with the paddle attachment, mix the yeast, milk, and sugar until dissolved, then cover and let rest for at least 10 minutes. Now add the shortening and salt. Beat on low speed until combined. Replace the mixer's paddle with a dough hook. Gradually add the flour, cup by cup, and bring it together until it forms a dough, then increase the speed and knead for another couple of minutes. Now place the ball of dough in a bowl lightly coated with oil. Cover and let rest in a warm spot for a couple of hours, until the dough doubles in size.

To make the jam, in a saucepan, combine the blueberries, honey, and lemon juice. Crush the blueberries with the back of a spoon—this will speed things up. Cook on medium heat for 20 to 25 minutes, until the jam starts to thicken. Let cool.

When you're ready to fry the toutons, heat the oil and butter in a skillet over medium heat. Punch the dough down in the bowl. Pull off chunks (about ½ cup each), flatten them between your hands into a rough puck shape, and place in the pan, leaving an inch between each touton. Flip the toutons as they begin to firm up, until both sides are golden brown and they're cooked through. Serve warm with butter.

LEFTOVER PASTA PIE

The other night, I was reading *The Gruffalo* to Sam in bed. By which I mean, every night I read him *The Gruffalo*. It's the book we always read after another three or four, the last book before he falls asleep.

One thing I hadn't expected after we adopted Sam was how fast I'd forget the fact of the adoption. He is our boy, and we are his daddies. When he falls asleep as I'm midway through *The Gruffalo* for the hundredth time, I'll sometimes lie there with him for the next half hour, not wanting to move and disturb him, and feeling amazed at how lucky I am. Okay, no, we aren't his biological parents, but in every other respect we are his family and he is ours. We haven't had a big discussion with him about the fact that he's adopted—he's still young, let's wait until he's got a bigger vocabulary—but he does recognize that other kids in his class have mommies and daddies, while he has two daddies. That doesn't seem to faze him. It just is what it is. That said, one day a year ago, he stopped on the walk home from school and told me that one girl in his room has two mommies, and made a can-you-believe-it face. But he was mostly impressed.

Someday he'll want to know more about his biological parents. Every adoption story is different, and the reasons that the child was removed from their birth parents, or given up by them, almost always involves thick layers upon layers of tragedy. The caseworkers at the Children's Aid Society didn't have much information about Sam's birth parents to share with us, other than they were young and not a couple, and not ready to raise him. It's the Children's Aid Society's policy to try their best to facilitate what they call "ethnic matches." Their theory is that a kid who looks like his or her adoptive parents, and comes from a similar culture, will have an easier time in life. At first, that policy seemed to me misguided: why should an ethnic match be more important than if the adoptive parent is good and loving? But then the matching happened with us, and I can see how it should be an important factor, especially for kids being adopted at an age older than Sam was when he joined us.

What we do know about his birth parents is that one of them, like Stephen, has an Irish background, and the other, like me, has an Italian background. Maybe that explains why Sam showed an instant love for toutons. And why he'd happily have pasta for dinner seven nights a week. I've caught him breaking into the pantry and pulling out uncooked strands of spaghetti to chew on. We don't make pasta quite every night, but it's often enough. Usually there's none left over, not after Sam has had his second and third plateful. But sometimes I'll make extra, and maybe double the recipe, because I have a craving for a leftover pasta pie for the next morning's breakfast. Sam craves pasta pie too. It's how I know he's my boy.

SERVES 4

• •

4 eggs

1 pound (or thereabouts) leftover spaghetti or linguine
   in a light tomato sauce

1 cup grated mozzarella, divided

1 cup freshly grated parmesan, divided

1 teaspoon pepper

1 tablespoon butter

1 tablespoon olive oil

• •

Preheat the oven to 375°F.

In a mixing bowl, beat the eggs, then add the pasta, ½ cup mozzarella, ½ cup parmesan, and the pepper, stirring to combine.

In an oven-safe skillet over medium heat, heat the butter and oil. Tip the pasta mixture into the pan and cook, undisturbed, for 5 minutes. Sprinkle the remaining ½ cup mozzarella and ½ cup parmesan on top of the pasta and transfer the pan to the oven. Bake for 10 to 15 minutes, until the cheese has formed a crust.

CHIVE AND PORK POT-STICKERS

During the first year of the pandemic, it seemed like everyone taught themselves to make bread. Sam and I wanted to master dumplings instead. We missed our regular Sunday trips to the warehouse-size dim sum palaces in Toronto's outer suburbs. The places with the best cheung fun and stuffed crab claw also seemed to be the noisiest and most chaotic, which meant our chaotic little family would never cause a disturbance. What we missed the most were the pot-stickers.

To prepare, we studied YouTube videos of home chefs and I reread *Land of Plenty* by the revered Sichuan food enthusiast Fuchsia Dunlop. Making dumplings at home turned out to be much less time-consuming than I'd expected, and didn't even require anything in the way of special equipment, though a stand mixer is a big help. It takes a few attempts to get the right consistency of dough, and if this is your first go it'll take a while to get the hang of folding the dumplings so they look relatively uniform. The technique is close to what we had to master to make Blueberry Pierogi (page 107), and in both instances my four-year-old had a more natural talent for forming the perfect crimp. Homemade dumplings won't replace our trips to dim sum palaces, but these make a good holdover.

MAKES 2 DOZEN POT-STICKERS

• •

For the wrappers

2 cups all-purpose flour

⅔ cup warm water (boil a kettle, then let the water cool to 120°F)

For the filling

1 pound ground pork

1 tablespoon cornstarch, mixed with ¼ cup water

2 tablespoons minced fresh ginger

1 tablespoon minced garlic

½ cup thinly sliced chives

1 teaspoon light sesame oil

1 tablespoon light soy sauce

1 tablespoon rice wine

1 teaspoon salt

1 teaspoon pepper

For frying and serving

Vegetable oil, for frying

1½ cups room-temperature water

1 cup light soy sauce, for serving

1 tablespoon sriracha, for serving

• •

To make the wrappers, place the flour in the bowl of a stand mixer. Slowly pour the water into the flour and, at the slowest speed, combine. Once the dough starts to come together, increase to medium speed and let the mixer work the dough for 3 minutes. Remove the dough from the mixer, form it into a ball, cover it in plastic wrap, and let it rest for half an hour. Knead the dough in the mixer again, then let it rest again, covered, for another half hour.

While the dough is resting, make the filling. In a bowl, mix the pork with the cornstarch slurry. Add the ginger, garlic, chives, sesame oil, soy sauce, rice wine, salt, and pepper and stir until well combined. Cover the bowl and leave the mixture to mellow for half an hour in the fridge.

It's time to start assembling. First step: sprinkle some flour on the dough. Using the palms of your hands, roll it out on a floured surface into a long rope that's not quite 2 inches thick. Cut the rope into 24 pieces, each 1 inch thick. Work with six of the pieces at a time, and cover the rest with plastic wrap—they dry quickly. Now use a well-floured rolling pin to roll each of the six pieces into a circle with a diameter of no more than 4 inches. Set aside, cover with plastic wrap, and repeat the process until you've got 24 circles.

Now it's time to fill and shape the dumplings—again, you'll want to do only six at a time, and then cover the formed dumplings with plastic wrap. Start by placing a tablespoon of the filling in each wrapper. Fold the wrappers over, forming a crescent shape, and pinch the edges together.

Once all your dumplings are formed, heat the cooking oil in a large skillet on medium-high heat. Working in batches, fry a dozen of the dumplings. Once they've started to brown on one side, pour the room-temperature water into the pan, lower the heat to medium, and cover the skillet with a heavy lid. In about 7 to 10 minutes the water will have largely evaporated. Now remove the lid and let the dumplings crisp up—another 1 or 2 minutes. Serve with soy sauce and sriracha for dipping.

STRAWBERRY-RHUBARB COBBLER

By midsummer, when we kids had run out of reruns to watch and finished every level of our video games and it was too hot to ride our bikes or kick a ball, Mom drew up a list of activities to get us out of the house and give her a few moments of quiet. Mostly this involved off-loading us onto our grandparents. My paternal grandparents, who spent all summer golfing, would bring us along as their personal caddies. Once they took us to the mall after a round, still dressed in our knee-length, pastel-plaid golf shorts and collared shirts, like rejects from the Osmond family singers. Of course, we immediately bumped into school friends. This, we decided, was true suffering.

Then, another summer day, Mom informed us that our other grandmother, her own mom, would be over soon to pick us up. She told us to put on our grubby clothes, meaning anything that wasn't our golf outfits. She wouldn't tell us why—it was a surprise. It'd be fun, don't worry. We didn't trust her. Grandma pulled up in her Firebird convertible and instructed us to sit with her in the front. The back seat was stacked with rows of wooden and cardboard baskets. We were going strawberry picking. Even more baskets waited in the trunk.

The pick-your-own farm was just outside the city. The rows of strawberry plants looked the same to me, but Grandma led us back and forth until she found a spot that looked relatively pristine. Okay, she said, let's get picking. The size didn't much matter, since the plan was to make jam, but we'd fill the baskets faster with bigger berries. The only problem was that all the berries were tiny—this day was going to take us forever. After half an hour we were ready to quit. The sun was high in the sky and the field was starting to broil around us. Can't we go home?

Okay, Grandma said, I've got a game: every time one of you fills a basket, you can have one strawberry. That sounded fair enough. We picked up the pace, and a few hours later filled all the baskets—there must have been 30 or 40. We hauled them back to the Firebird and flopped into the front seat. We'd be glad to never see another strawberry field again. Grandma had lunch waiting for us back at her place. I promise, she said, there's no strawberries on the menu.

We complained and complained about how Mom had sent us strawberry picking. Summer was supposed to be about bikes and swimming and fun, not being sent to work. A week later, when Grandma dropped off a dozen jars of strawberry jam, we changed our minds. The jam jars seemed to glow a ruby red from within. The jam itself was sugary and tart all at once—like nothing we'd ever tried from a store. The next summer, we asked Grandma when she wanted to go again.

I'm looking forward to taking Sam strawberry picking someday, when there's less of a chance he'll impulsively bolt for the nearest tractor. For now, we've made some quick jams with berries from a roadside stand. We've also baked fresh-picked strawberries in a cobbler. Baking concentrates the berries' flavour, as if you've added a cup of caramel. In this recipe, I've provided a variation that replaces two cups of berries with rhubarb, for anyone who finds strawberries on their own a little too sweet.

SERVES 4 TO 6

● ●

1 cup granulated sugar, divided

2 tablespoons cornstarch

3 cups hulled and halved
strawberries

2 cups rhubarb (only the red
parts), cut into 1-inch pieces

1 cup all-purpose flour

1 teaspoon baking powder

Pinch of salt

7 tablespoons butter, divided

½ cup whipping cream

● ●

Preheat the oven to 350°F.

In a large bowl, mix ½ cup sugar and the cornstarch. Add the fruit, toss
to coat, and set aside.

In a second, medium bowl, whisk together the flour, remaining sugar,
baking powder, and salt. Cut 6 tablespoons butter into small pieces and
tip into the dry ingredients. Using your fingers, rub the butter and dry
ingredients together. After a few minutes it'll form a coarse mixture.
(When you're about halfway there, it's a good moment to get a kid
involved in hand mixing.) Gradually pour in the cream and, using
a wooden spoon, mix to combine into a rough batter.

On the stovetop, melt the remaining tablespoon of butter in the skillet.
Pour in the fruit mixture and let it bubble away for a couple of minutes.
Then spoon the batter on top, distributing the clumps evenly. There'll be
gaps in a few places, which is a good thing (it allows the steam from the
cooking fruit to escape and for the fruit juices to mingle with the cobbler
topping). Transfer to the oven and bake for 30 to 35 minutes, until the top
is golden and the fruit is bubbling through.

SUNDAY
48

PLAIN FRENCH TOAST

Plain French toast always puts me in a romantic mood. I can see that it's
maybe just a little weird to be talking about romance in a book about
eating with family. But I'm thinking of romance in the broadest sense: the
romance of being loved. The romance of French toast is a key plot point
in our family story. It's toast, it's French (but actually Roman, maybe), it's
romantically delicious. Also deliciously romantic. Hear me out.

Before Stephen, I'd convinced myself I'd given up on finding that guy
who rom-coms tell us is called The One. I was pretty sure I'd vetted all the
eligible guys in Toronto. Using the same researcher-journalist-amateur-
sociologist approach I brought to everything, I'd been very deliberate at
sorting and classifying all the gay guys in my age cohort in the city. Maybe
300 of them? They were either too uptight or too easygoing. Too sporty or
too sedentary. They drank too much or they smoked. They liked terrible
music or, worse, didn't listen to any music. Then there were the guys who
were even more cynical than me and spent every night cycling through
the gay bars, intent on never connecting with anyone for more than a
moment. Not one of them was right, or the ones who were probably right

were already taken (the universal plight of the rom-com protagonist). Most guys I knew were better as friends, I decided as I sat in my apartment watching *Gilmore Girls* reruns with my longtime roommate. Catherine and I started to make vague plans about buying a house (she was also in a romance rut) so we could at least have a backyard to grow some vegetables as we grew old together.

Then one night a school friend wanted me to meet him at a dance club, because what else was there to do? I mostly kept to the back wall, waiting for songs we liked. After an hour I was ready to leave. Then this guy walked in with a couple of friends. He had shaggy gingerish hair and a big smile, and was wearing long shorts that were either a bad fashion choice or proof he didn't care much about what people thought. I'd never seen him before—he hadn't been sorted or categorized. Maybe he was a tourist? I decided to stick around longer. After another pint, I sidled up and introduced myself. Hi, he smiled, I'm Stephen.

French toast happened two weeks later. We'd exchanged phone numbers and promised to meet for a movie, but our schedules never seemed to match up. Then Stephen proposed something I'd never heard anyone propose before: I should come by his place the next day for breakfast. I was so surprised, I believe I blurted out a yes. He lived in a neighbourhood that today is dense with condos, but back then was most notable for a bread factory and empty parking lots. His apartment was what real estate agents now call a "hard loft," meaning it was a rough space a landlord had carved out of a former munitions factory. It had iron windows looking into a courtyard, a bedroom area reached by a rickety ladder, and a skylight above the bed that he had to cover with a sheet because other people in the building had a lot of parties on the roof. It was a bit rough and temporary-looking, but I was impressed that he had his own place. He asked me to wait on the couch while he got breakfast going. That's when I clocked the bowl of cut fruit on the table and the two place settings with linen napkins. He set to work slicing up a baguette and whisking eggs. It was dawning on me that he'd put some serious planning into this breakfast, and I'd shown up on my bike expecting maybe a bowl of cereal. He was making me French toast! Who the hell was this guy?

That morning was followed by many more French toast breakfasts. It was, I'd say, around the fifth breakfast together (by that point I was staying overnight) that I stopped to imagine what it'd be like if this became more than a guy for the moment. In his bed, staring up at that sheet-covered skylight while he was below whisking eggs, I realized I had to take this seriously. I thought through the next steps: one of us would need to propose living together and we'd have to combine our things and throw out duplicate whisks and spatulas; we'd get a dog and at some point we'd realize we needed a car to haul the bags of dog food; then, if all went well, there'd be a house and vacations and introductions to his parents and my parents, and throwing birthday parties, attending funerals together, combined bank accounts, and life insurance policies. Would we get married? I'd heard about some gay couples who were raising kids. Would we do that?

Then Stephen called me down. Breakfast was ready. I sat in my chair and started working on a slice of French toast. I asked Stephen what it was about his French toast that made it so good—other than, you know, it was made by him. Well, he said, looking a little flustered, it's better if the bread is stale. The whole point of French toast, he went on, is to take something that you might throw out, but is still perfectly good, and make it new again.

I decided then, though kept it to myself, that I'd put the plan in motion. A few months later, I asked Stephen to move in.

What follows are four recipes for French toast: the classic version, plus three variations. The secret to good French toast is—always—that the bread be a bit stale. Day-old is good for baguette, a couple of days old for challah or other soft breads. Part of the appeal—and, yes, the romance—of

French toast is that the basic recipe allows for experimentation, so it never gets boring. My favourite remains exactly how Stephen made it years ago, in his loft in the munitions factory, the only frill a dollop of whipped cream on top.

SERVES 3 TO 4

• •

1 large day-old baguette

4 eggs

½ cup milk

1 cup whipping cream, divided

1 teaspoon vanilla paste

½ teaspoon cinnamon

Butter, for frying

1 tablespoon granulated sugar

• •

Slice the baguette on the bias, so each piece has more surface area. In a mixing bowl, whisk together the eggs, milk, ½ cup cream, vanilla, and cinnamon.

In a skillet over medium heat, heat the butter. Soak the bread in the egg mixture, then fry until both sides are browned. (Depending on how many pieces you can fit in your skillet, you might want to keep batches warm on a pan in an oven set to 300°F.)

In another mixing bowl, whisk the remaining ½ cup cream and the sugar until you have soft peaks. Stack the cooked French toast on plates and spoon the whipped cream on top.

STUFFED FRENCH TOAST

This is my attempt at a hybrid recipe, combining French toast and that other great necessity of life, a croque monsieur. The mustard is optional—and probably a bad idea if you're feeding a kid who objects to anything with a kick of heat. We often make this if we're having a late weekend breakfast. Sometimes we'll have had it for breakfast and, a few hours later, Sam will ask if we can have it again for lunch.

SERVES 4

6 eggs

1½ cups milk

1 loaf day-old crusty white bread

3 teaspoons Dijon (optional)

8 slices Black Forest ham

8 slices cheese (a mild, semi-hard cheese like Comté, edam, or Jarlsberg is ideal)

Butter, for frying

In a bowl, whisk the eggs and milk, then set aside.

Slice eight pieces of bread (they should each be 1½ to 2 inches thick).
Cut open a pocket into one side of each piece: imagine you're slicing open
a pita bread and, using a sharp, serrated knife (I usually use a steak knife),
saw along the length of the bread slice without breaking the other three
sides. The pocket needs to be deep enough to hold the ham and cheese.
Spread some mustard on the ham, then slip a slice each of the ham and
cheese into the pocket.

In a skillet over medium-low heat, heat the butter. Dip both faces of the
stuffed bread into the egg mixture. Fry the bread, flipping once, until
golden brown on both sides and the cheese inside has melted and is
starting to ooze out.

SUNDAY

50

COCONUT-MANGO FRENCH TOAST

It's a strange day in our house if a loaf of challah doesn't disappear in
a few hours. When I'm planning for this recipe, I'll make a point of buying
an extra loaf and hiding it somewhere extra sneaky, like in the shelf of
the closet where Sam never finds the time to hang his coats. The coconut
added to the egg dip will crisp up as the French toast browns, adding extra
crunch to the plush challah. I use desiccated instead of shredded coconut
because it's drier and so crisps up faster, plus the shorter flakes bind better
to the bread. It also goes extremely well with the accompanying mango
dipping sauce.

SERVES 4

• •

1 tablespoon granulated sugar

1 ripe Haden mango or 2 ripe Alphonso mangoes,
    chopped into ¼-inch cubes

2 tablespoons water

6 eggs

1½ cups milk

1 teaspoon vanilla paste

½ teaspoon cinnamon

½ cup desiccated coconut

1 loaf day-old challah

Butter, for frying

• •

In a small pot, combine the sugar, mangoes, and water. Simmer until the mangoes have fully collapsed, stirring occasionally. Remove from the heat, mash the mango pieces with the back of a fork, and set aside to cool.

In a mixing bowl, whisk together the eggs, milk, vanilla, and cinnamon. Add the coconut and stir to combine. Slice eight pieces of challah (they should each be about 1½ inches thick).

In a skillet over medium-low heat, heat the butter. Soak each side of the bread in the egg mixture. Fry the bread, flipping once, until golden brown on both sides and the coconut is crisp. Plate and top with the mango sauce.

EGGNOG FRENCH TOAST BAKE

A second cousin to French toast is that comfy-cozy English dessert of bread pudding. Both require a lot of eggs, though for the pudding they're in service of a custard. And instead of frying, a pudding gets baked or steamed. In this recipe I take advantage of two things that are always in our house come Christmastime: eggnog and panettone. Panettone is similar to brioche in that both are enriched with eggs and sugar. But because panettone is left to rise for a few days (versus a few hours for brioche), it has more airy volume and absorbs whatever you spread or pour on it. That's also what makes panettone ideal for this pudding-style bake.

SERVES 4 TO 6

• •

2½ cups eggnog

¼ cup granulated sugar

3 eggs

1 teaspoon vanilla paste

¼ teaspoon salt

1 panettone (2 pounds)

½ cup Nutella (optional)

½ cup roughly chopped pecans (optional)

¼ cup candied orange peel (optional)

¼ cup powdered sugar

• •

The night before you plan to make this, slice the panettone into 3-inch wedges. Spread evenly on a baking sheet. Leave uncovered and somewhere out of reach of small (and big) hands. You want the bread to dry out overnight.

The next morning, preheat the oven to 350°F. Grease a 9 × 12-inch cake pan with butter and set aside.

In a mixing bowl, whisk together the eggnog, granulated sugar, eggs, vanilla, and salt. Arrange the panettone wedges in one snug layer in the baking sheet. Pour the eggnog mixture overtop and leave to soak for 10 minutes. Drop teaspoons of Nutella in spots where there are gaps between the bread, and scatter the pecans across the top of the bread.

Bake for 30 minutes or until the top is golden brown. Just before serving, sprinkle with the optional candied orange peel and dust with powdered sugar.

KRINGEL (CHRISTMAS BREAD)

When it comes to Christmas, I'm a sentimentalist. Stephen is less charitable: he calls me a sap. The day after Halloween, I start playing the Vince Guaraldi Trio's *A Charlie Brown Christmas* album and plan how I'll string the lights on the house, the theme for the tree, and a schedule of dinners that'll keep apart relatives who'd rather not mix.

As a kid, like most kids, I was certain my family was weird in most respects, especially around the holidays. We placed presents under the Christmas tree and all that rigmarole, but the adults plainly viewed the entire month as a sentence to be endured rather than the magical time as sold to me by cartoons and my kindergarten teacher. The men would sit silently in the rec room watching James Bond marathons, while the women would enforce peace among the cousins. Sooner or later I recognized that we weren't unique—no one's family gets along and everyone watches Bond as an avoidance technique. And I realized that, even though everyone resented the forced togetherness, no one complained about the food, which was always excellent. For Sam, I decided to recreate those prolonged hours stuck inside with relatives, in particular the warmth of a kitchen after a full day of cooking and the feasting hours around the dining table, every available extension leaf put to use.

The guest list at our holiday table includes my mom and grandma, who always wear matching Christmas sweaters, Stephen's opera singer brother and his partner, and a random assortment of however many friends or family are in town. One year, Catherine, now a parent with two red-headed girls, joined us; another, it was Sam's honorary gay uncles. For the menu I follow the bird-and-stuffing orthodoxy. A couple of Christmases ago I tried a goose, but the fat splatter made a holy mess, and white meat fans were left hungry. I now swear by turkeys raised on a Mennonite farm near our city. I usually make a stuffing with wild boar sausage and pecans, and for the sides I sweeten my roasted yams with maple syrup and, at the last minute, sauté shredded brussels sprouts with pancetta. I'm not allowed to make the gravy. Stephen is finicky about the consistency. He spends forever simmering down the turkey drippings and pressing the results through a sieve until it's as silky as custard and ideal for pouring onto leftovers in the days ahead.

The one recipe that defines the holidays for me is kringel, an enriched Nordic bread that's braided and gets its distinctive flavour and deep yellow hue from saffron and cardamom. My Estonian grandmother calls it "sai," three letters that are surprisingly impossible to correctly pronounce if you're not used to a Finno-Ugric tangle of vowels. It's like challah or brioche, but denser and more elaborately braided, studded with almonds and raisins, and dusted with powdered sugar. I like to toast a slice and smear it with butter or rhubarb jam. My grandmother's kringel is my pinnacle. She bakes it from memory from *Eesti Kokaraamat*, a 1976 cookbook that compiled recipes from Estonian expats. Kringel is also very close to a braided Finnish bread called pulla, which I've brought home from a nearby Finnish bistro. Theirs is good, but not as good as my grandmother's. Lucky for me, she still bakes kringel for our birthdays and big holidays. Without it, Christmas wouldn't be the same.

We'll have it for dessert with dinner, but the best time to have it is with Christmas Day breakfast, maybe with a plate of eggs and bacon. But it does well on its own, and, let's be real, few parents have the will power to cook breakfast on Christmas morning, and few kids really care either way—they're too eager to open and play with presents. So I brew a big pot of coffee and slice us each a few pieces of kringel, which we spread with butter and jam.

I've adapted my kringel recipe from grandma's copy of *Eesti Kokaraamat*. The instructions appear simple, but much depends on trial and error, especially with your braiding technique. It's better to let the dough rise on a humid day. Fresher yeast also helps. My grandmother also swears it only turns out right if she bakes it in a festive mood, perhaps while sipping some rum and eggnog.

The bread stays fresh for three or four days. It also freezes well—slice before you freeze it, and then toast individual pieces straight from the freezer. Fresh bread doesn't need toasting, but either way it goes well with red berry jams or butter. I sometimes double the recipe and make two loaves, since I like to have some around for as long as the holidays last.

MAKES 1 SUBSTANTIAL LOAF

• •

2 cups milk

1½ tablespoons active dry yeast

2 to 4 threads saffron

8 tablespoons butter

1 cup granulated sugar

3 eggs, divided

Pinch of salt

1 teaspoon cardamom

Zest of 1 orange

8 cups all-purpose flour

1 cup golden raisins

1 tablespoon water

½ cup blanched and slivered almonds

¼ cup powdered sugar

• •

⟿▶

In a small saucepan over medium heat, warm the milk to 110°F—a kitchen thermometer is helpful here. In the bowl of a stand mixer with a paddle attachment, dissolve the yeast in the milk. Leave for 10 minutes. Add the saffron threads and leave to soak for another 2 minutes. Add the butter, sugar, and two eggs, and beat to combine. Replace the paddle with a bread hook. Now add the salt, cardamom, and orange zest. Gradually add the flour, cup by cup, with the mixer on the lowest setting. Combine until it forms a dough. Increase to the medium setting and knead for 10 minutes or until the dough is elastic. Add the raisins. Cover with a damp tea towel and leave the bowl to rest in a warm spot until the dough has doubled in size—about 3 hours.

Preheat the oven to 350°F. Line a baking sheet with parchment paper.

On a floured surface, divide the dough into three balls. Roll each ball into a rope about 3 inches thick. Now comes the fun (i.e., tricky) part. If you've ever braided hair, you'll know exactly what to do. Line the three ropes closely together at one end, with the rope gradually spreading apart. Lift and drape the left rope over the middle rope so it rests between the middle and the right rope. Then do the same with the right rope, resting it between the middle and the left. Repeat this lifting and draping until you reach the end, then tuck the ends of the ropes together.

Place the braided bread on the prepared baking sheet. Beat the remaining egg with a tablespoon of water, and brush the top surface of the bread with the egg wash. Stick the almond slivers into the bread so they point out at a 45-degree angle. Bake the bread for 30 minutes, until the crust is golden brown. Let cool on a wire rack, then dust with the powdered sugar.

ACKNOWLEDGEMENTS

I'm lucky that I've never found the writer's life lonely. Rebecca Philps, Craig Baines, and Alec Scott read early drafts and helped point me where I needed to go. Anita and Prajakt Samant mailed me beautiful cookbooks. My cheerleading squad and frequent dining companions include Carley Fortune, Mark Hayward, Malcolm Johnston, Peter Kingstone, Emily Landau, Amrita Mathur, Marco Posadas, Courtney Shea, Catherine Stinson, and Cindy Wan.

I'm grateful to everyone at Appetite, especially Robert McCullough and my editors, Rachel Brown and Bhavna Chauhan. Copyeditor Lana Okerlund buffed these pages to a perfect polish. My always astute agent Jackie Kaiser told me that this, not those dozen other book ideas, was the one.

John Montgomery helped vet illustrators and introduced me to the extraordinary Christopher Rouleau, who painted the cutest-ever Pyrex measuring cup, plus 11 more irreverent artworks. Jenna Marie Wakani captured the most flattering light in our kitchen.

Any skill I have as a writer I picked up as a magazine editor. Sarah Fulford, Angie Gardos, and Rachel Heinrichs gave me the opportunity to write about food, and dine on their dime, for *Toronto Life*. A version of "Sunday 52: Kringel (Christmas Bread)" first appeared in that magazine. At *Chatelaine*, Carolyn Chua showed me how to test a recipe until it's foolproof. I miss daily cake with Gillian Grace, Sun Ngo, Kathryn Hayward, and Maureen Halushak. Gary Stephen Ross hired me at *Saturday Night* and became a lifelong mentor.

My biggest debts are to my mother, Helen, and grandmothers, Oie and Audry.

SOURCES

3   *kids do better at school:* Adolphus et al., "The effects of breakfast on behavior and academic performance in children and adolescents," *Frontiers in Human Neuroscience.*

3   *one Australian meta-analysis:* Oforio-Asenso et al., "Skipping breakfast and the risk of cardiovascular disease and death: A systematic review of prospective cohort studies in primary prevention settings," *Journal of Cardiovascular Development and Disease.*

3   *the family table was originally a sacrificial altar:* Kaufmann, *The Meaning of Cooking.*

3   *the mass popularization of gastronomy:* Gopnik, *The Table Comes First.*

10   *mix-up of sensations:* Grandin, *The Autistic Brain: Helping Different Kinds of Minds Succeed;* Prizant, *Uniquely Human: A Different Way of Seeing Autism;* Rogers et al., *An Early Start for Your Child with Autism.*

12   *minds away from temptations:* Arndt Anderson, *Breakfast: A History.*

12   *French toast isn't actually French:* Fass, *Around the Roman Table: Food and Fasting in Ancient Rome.*

27   *were invented by the British:* Arndt Anderson, *Breakfast: A History.*

28   *why toasted bread is browned:* Martins et al., "A review of Maillard reaction in food and implications to kinetic modelling," *Trends in Food Science and Technology.*

38   *avocado toast is rich in B vitamins:* Fulgoni et al., "Avocado consumption is associated with better diet quality and nutrient intake, and lower metabolic syndrome risk in U.S. adults," *Nutrition Journal.*

38   *the most recognizable variety, the Hass:* Wells, *Lives of the Trees: An Uncommon History.*

58   *the Ashkenazi original:* Weinzweig, "The secret history of bagels," *The Atlantic.*

63   *cupcakes and American-style muffins:* Simmons, *American Cookery.*

64   *under the amazing name Mmmuffins:* Gould, *The New Entrepreneurs: 80 Canadian Success Stories.*

70   *those 1980s cookbook icons:* Rosso and Lukins, *The New Basics Cookbook.*

76   *a dish called toad in a hole:* Lucraft, "General satisfaction: A history of baked puddings," *The English Kitchen: Historical Essays.*

79   *shakshuka, the Tunisian dish:* Ottolenghi and Tamimi, *Jerusalem: A Cookbook.*

82   *with many temples to build and battles to wage:* Arndt Anderson, *Breakfast: A History.*

82   *hosting his daybreak guests:* Pepys, "Tuesday, January 1, 1660/61," *The Diary of Samuel Pepys.*

83   *Charles Ranhofer, a chef at Delmonico's:* Claiborne, "American classic: Eggs Benedict," *The New York Times.*

89   *Corning casserole dish:* Yardley, "S. Donald Stookey, scientist, dies at 99; among his inventions was CorningWare," *The New York Times.*

94   *by virtue of being so dry and plain:* Arndt Anderson, *Breakfast: A History.*

100 *reads like a handbook for the 1 percent:* Bailey, *Country Weekends: Recipes for Good Food and Easy Living.*

103 *needed a healthy breakfast for his patients:* Arndt Anderson, *Breakfast: A History.*

103 a granola-like breakfast cereal called muesli: Gratzer, *Terrors of the Table: The Curious History of Nutrition.*

124 *the California restaurant that influenced a thousand other restaurants:* Bertolli, *Chez Panisse Cooking.*

127 *created the Egg McMuffin:* Kroc and Anderson, *Grinding It Out: The Making of McDonald's.*

130 *the first mass-manufactured waffle iron:* Kindy, "A brief history of the waffle iron," *Smithsonian Magazine.*

143 *a shortcut cassoulet recipe:* Olson, *Living High off the Hog: Over 100 Recipes and Techniques to Cook Pork Perfectly.*

151 *the U.S. military air-dropped two million:* Colin and Pott, *The Blue Pages.*

151 *two-foot-high flames shot out:* Michaud, "Strawberry Pop-Tart blow-torches."

177 *toutons should be served hot:* Story et al. (Eds.), *Dictionary of Newfoundland English.*

183 *revered Sichuan food enthusiast:* Dunlop, *Land of Plenty: A Treasury of Authentic Sichuan Cooking.*

While researching and cooking with Sam, I found inspiration in *James Beard's American Cookery*; Abigail Carroll's *Three Squares: The Invention of the American Meal*; Pauline Carter's *The Great Nova Scotia Cookbook*; Laurie Colwin's *Home Cooking: A Writer in the Kitchen*; all of M.F.K. Fisher, especially *The Gastronomical Me*; Rachel Giese's *Boys: What It Means to Become a Man*; Michael Harris's *All We Want: Building the Life We Cannot Buy*; Daniel Isengart's *The Art of Gay Cooking*; Mark and Talia Kurlansky's *International Night: A Father and Daughter Cook Their Way around the World*; Karen Page and Andrew Dornenburg's *The Flavor Bible: The Essential Guide to Culinary Creativity, Based on the Wisdom of America's Most Imaginative Chefs*; all of Nigel Slater, especially *The Christmas Chronicles: Notes, Stories and 100 Essential Recipes for Midwinter*; and, Anne Willan's *Women in the Kitchen: Twelve Essential Cookbook Writers Who Defined the Way We Eat, from 1661 to Today.*

INDEX